MAXIMIZING PROFITS IN SMALL AND MEDIUM-SIZED BUSINESSES

Jerome D. Braverman

VAN NOSTRAND REINHOLD COMPANY
NEW YORK   CINCINNATI   TORONTO   LONDON   MELBOURNE

Copyright © 1984 by Van Nostrand Reinhold Company Inc.

Library of Congress Catalog Card Number: 83-10414
ISBN: 0-442-21268-2

Manufactured in the United States of America

Published by Van Nostrand Reinhold Company Inc.
135 West 50th Street, New York, N.Y. 10020

Van Nostrand Reinhold
480 Latrobe Street
Melbourne, Victoria 3000, Australia

Van Nostrand Reinhold Company Limited
Molly Millars Lane
Wokingham, Berkshire, England

15 14 13 12 11 10 9 8 7 6 5 4 3 2 1

Library of Congress Cataloging in Publication Data
Braverman, Jerome D.
  Maximizing profits in small and medium-sized
businesses.

  Includes index.
  1. Small business—Management. I. Title.
HD62.7.B72   1983   658′.022   83-10414
ISBN 0-442-21268-2

To Millie,
for a multitude of reasons

Preface

"Businesses fail because managers fail. The successful company is managed by the individual who makes a minimum of blunders." So says Tobias C. Carbone, President of T and R Enterprises and Associate Professor of Economics and Business Administration at Illinois College in an article in *Management Week*. He cites failure to plan, ineffective staffing, poor money management, and sloppy record keeping as the four most common failures of managers. Whether or not these are actually the four most common causes of business failure is irrelevant. Businesses do fail frequently, and in the final analysis the failures are due to an inability to sustain adequate profits. All four factors just mentioned lead to profit erosion, and profit erosion leads to business failure.

The responsibility for profit erosion falls upon the manager. Whether he is the entrepreneur and owner of a firm, the chief executive officer, or the manager of a division or department, the manager must assume the responsibility for those factors that erode profits and eventually lead to failure. It's easy to refer to management blunders, but those blunders are usually the result, not of carelessness, but of a lack of knowledge. Most managers have a large store of specialized knowledge because it is their expertise in a particular field that enabled them to attain the position of manager in the first place. But as they progress upward in the management heirarchy, or reach a point where they are ready to branch out on their own, they realize, or should realize, that specialized knowledge in one field simply isn't sufficient to assure success in business. Business with all of its varied functions is simply too complicated. At that point what is needed is a breadth of knowledge and experience across specialties and fields that most managers have not had the opportunity to acquire. And that's when the blunders start. The successful manager who operates the successful business overcomes this lack. The unsuccessful manager doesn't.

Business periodicals are replete with stories of phenomenal business successes and failures. Of course, we hear a great deal more about the former than we do about the latter. The fact remains, however, that the failures far outnumber the successes, particularly among small businesses.

Nowhere are successes and failures more spectacular than in the glamorous high technology fields. One need only recall the advent of semiconductors in the sixties and an early starter with tremendous prospects named Transitron. In every new field there comes time for a shakeout. When the chips are down, those companies with good product and good management survive while others with equally good product but poor management fail. Transitron didn't make it.

It is seldom possible to pinpoint a single cause of business failure because it is seldom the result of a single catastrophic occurrence or one bad decision. Business failure results from the cumulative effect of many bad decisions, inefficiencies, and less than optimal practices over a period of time.

Contrast the record of Apple Computers with that of Transitron. Sales of this company—started in a garage workshop in 1976 by two young computer specialists—passed the $100 million mark in 1980. Steven P. Jobs, Chairman and co-founder, predicts sales of $1 billion by 1990. That may be possible, but there is bound to be a shakeout in the microcomputer business also. Whether Apple meets that prediction or goes down to failure will depend upon its ability to operate efficiently when the competition gets tough and the going gets rough. Although Apple has a good product and the microcomputer concept has captured the imagination of the public, Commodore, Atari, Radio Shack-Tandy, IBM, and others also have good products. How many of them will still be on the market by 1990?

Survival in the present business environment depends on providing a good product or service that is in demand. But doing so, though necessary, is in itself not sufficient. The business must also operate efficiently. Profits must be maximized. But profit is simply the difference between revenues and expenses. Regardless of how high revenues are, there will be no profit if expenses are higher.

Marketing has become a widely possessed skill. Marketing, advertising, merchandising, in fact, constitute the glamorous side of business. Nevertheless, profits are mainly determined in the less glamorous areas of operating efficiencies. Cutting costs is where profits are made today, and cutting or minimizing costs requires specialized knowledge and tools in many diverse business activities. The application of these tools to the common sources of profit erosion is what is required to maximize profits. Without them, the manager will flounder if he tries to explain to himself, his bosses, or his board of directors why—even though sales have never been better—profits are declining. The purpose of this book is to provide the manager with the knowledge and tools that he needs to maximize profits.

Beginning with a simple checklist to help him locate the sources of profit erosion, the book proceeds to describe methods for minimizing costs in the most common areas where profit erosion occurs—in inventories, purchasing, production control, and so on. It also discusses the indispensable tools every manager needs: forecasting techniques, breakeven analysis, and management information systems. No book can guarantee to make a manager effective, but it can go a long way to help him overcome deficiencies that may prevent him from being so. That is precisely what this book proposes to do.

JEROME D. BRAVERMAN

Contents

1. The Goal of Maximizing Profit

For most businesses in today's extremely competitive economy, profits appear increasingly difficult to achieve. And even when profits are realized, the state and federal governments manage to reduce them substantially through taxation. What remains for reinvestment and distribution to owners and investors usually falls far short of their original expectations. Nonetheless, a great deal of profit erosion results from operating inefficiencies within the business. These inefficiencies do not necessarily result from poor management per se but frequently stem from a lack of specific expertise in certain critical areas by managers who have multiple responsibilities.

It should be obvious that the primary purpose of any business operating in a free economy is to make a profit. Without profits, no business could survive. However, the objective of simply making a profit is not in itself sufficient for business success. In order to be successful, a business must *maximize* profit. That is, it must realize its total profit potential. No business, regardless of size, can afford to sacrifice profit to inefficiency in performing its necessary functions.

Newspapers and news and financial periodicals are replete with stories and statistics about business failures and bankruptcies. It is usually the small and medium-sized businesses that appear most subject to failure these days. However, recent developments in the news have shown that even billion dollar corporations are subject to the same factors that can lead to bankruptcy as smaller businesses and require massive outside assistance in order to avoid that fate.

Insufficient capital and lack of competence in one or more of the various functional areas necessary to the operation of any business are major causes of failure. There is nothing that we can or will suggest here to alleviate the first of those factors. But there are many things that can be done to eliminate the second, and these constitute the subject matter of this book.

Certain essential functions are common to all business enterprises whether the enterprise is a purveyor of goods or a supplier of services, a retailer, a wholesaler, or a manufacturer. These functions include, but are not necessarily limited to, purchasing, marketing, allocating and managing human and material resources, controlling inventories, assuring quality, and accounting for and controlling costs. In different guises and under different labels, these functions are required in all business enterprises. In large organizations, the various functional areas are staffed with experts, or at least specialists. At the other extreme—the one-person business—the owner must perform all these functions himself. In between are small to medium-sized businesses in which managers have multiple responsibilities and the chief executive more or less directly controls all functional areas. It is in these latter cases that specific expertise is lacking, inefficiencies occur, and profits are lost.

Even in large corporations where specialists are employed to perform these specific functions, a responsible executive cannot abrogate his responsibility for less than optimal results by placing the blame on his subordinates. Consequently the executive responsible for a profit center should be familiar enough with the functions performed by his subordinates to be able to exercise effective supervision and to troubleshoot when difficulties arise.

Operating any business involves certain risks, and many hazards confront the owner or manager trying to achieve his goals and objectives. However, many tools have been developed to help overcome these risks and hazards, and the more of these that the manager can use effectively, the more likely he can achieve those objectives. Frequently, the knowledge of and the ability to use the appropriate tools is the difference between success and failure. Of course, no individual can be expert in all the diverse functional areas of modern business operations. Nevertheless, even small inefficiencies and less than optimal decisions, if they recur frequently in day-to-day operations, can result in substantial increases in costs and reductions in profit. Much of this inefficiency results from a simple lack of knowledge or information about the techniques and tools used by specialists to optimize performance in these areas. Unfortunately, although most of these techniques are relatively simple and can be learned quite easily, they are not generally available from a single source and in a form which makes it easy for a manager or executive to acquire the knowledge necessary to apply them effectively. We will attempt to remedy this situation with what follows.

BUSINESS GOALS AND OBJECTIVES

In order to achieve maximum effectiveness in operating a business, the objectives of every functional unit must be consistent with the overall goals of the enterprise. However, unless an explicit effort is directed at establishing these goals and their appropriate priorities, it is often difficult to determine what the real goals actually are. It is even more difficult to assess the relative importance of multiple goals. And every enterprise has several goals of varying importance. First, there is the obvious goal of maximizing profit. However, there are other, less obvious goals such as growth, prominence, producing a high quality product or service, enhancing the company image or reputation, providing employment and opportunities for advancement to employees, and so on.

Whenever multiple goals and objectives exist, the achievement of some will likely conflict with the achievement of others. Furthermore, a business and its owners or managers do not exist and operate in a vacuum. In order to be successful the business must always satisfy other parties which have their own goals. These others include the potential customers who exchange money in return for the product or service offered by the business, the employees who exchange their services for wages, and the vendors who provide necessary materials, supplies, and services in return for monetary payments. The objectives of these parties and others must be satisfied simultaneously if the business is to prosper. However, before it can satisfy the goals of these others, the business must first survive as an economic institution. It must operate profitably. Consequently, the first and highest priority goal of the business must be to maximize profit.

Operationally, the owner or manager must make decisions on the basis of various functional imperatives. These are criteria by which the effectiveness of a particular function or transaction can be evaluated. The primary objective at the company level is of course profit maximization. As long as the functional objectives are consistent with the company objectives, the business should prosper and achieve its several purposes. However, functional objectives themselves may be in conflict, and it is not always easy to determine how the various functions should be performed to resolve these conflicts in a manner consistent with the overall company objective of profit maximization. In fact, resolving conflicting objectives is the major problem in profit maximization. Most such situations are not amenable to resolution by guesses, intuition or hunches.

Some additional remarks about the goal of maximizing profits appear to be appropriate here. Though this decision criterion seems to be clear at the company level, there are often difficulties in applying it to operational problems in the various functional areas of the business. Because of the many constituencies serving and served by the organization, some functional areas may address themselves to the needs and objectives of those constituencies, and decision-making criteria may be selected according to this particular orientation. When conflicts in several objectives arise they can sometimes be resolved by relating them explicitly to the higher level objectives. When this is insufficient or simply doesn't work, other methods must be used.

Of course, profit maximization as a primary goal of the business must or should entail some restrictions. The restrictions imposed and accepted differ from business to business, owner to owner, manager to manager. Most would adhere to the law of the land in achieving objectives, but some might not. Most would not market or distribute an unsafe product; others might. Some managements would close a branch operation with little or no notice; others would do so only after making substantial efforts to alleviate the problems which result from the closing. Restrictions such as these are a part of our society, and as the society changes, so do the restrictions.

Finally, some noneconomic decisions will undoubtedly be made by management. Certain employee benefits or customer services, or vendor courtesies, or community activities fall outside of strict economic considerations. To attribute these to profit maximization seems to be stretching the point. However, most economic problems should be resolved according to economic criteria. When conflicts arise between economic and noneconomic criteria, the methods of analysis presented here should resolve the economic problem. The noneconomic problems cannot be resolved so easily, yet these same methods can also help provide an economic evaluation of the decisions which result when noneconomic criteria are applied.

THE PRODUCTION SYSTEM

Think of a business as a production system. A production system can be defined as an arrangement of people, material, energy and facilities through which work is accomplished. Work is accomplished when materials are converted from one form to another, when people are served or treated, when information is processed, and when goods change hands. Every production system consists of three basic factors:

1. That which is worked on or with, called the *inputs*
2. The work that is performed, the *process*
3. That which is produced, called the *outputs*

Factor number 2, the process, converts the set of inputs into some desired set of outputs. In effect then a production system is the means by which resource inputs are transformed to create useful goods and services as outputs.

The inputs to the production system come in a wide variety of types and forms. In manufacturing systems, the principle inputs are raw material, energy, labor, machinery, facilities, information and technology. In service systems the inputs are dominated by labor, but, depending on the exact kind of system, machines, facilities, information and technology are also inputs in varying proportions. Of course, capital is the indispensable input in all types of production systems. Without capital, none of the other inputs would be possible. The actual conversion of inputs to outputs requires the application of technology as well as the management of all the variables in the system. Whether this transformation is accomplished efficiently or inefficiently depends greatly on the effectiveness of management.

The effectiveness of a production system can be measured and expressed in various ways. One common measure is *productivity*. Productivity is usually expressed as a ratio of output to input. Increasing productivity is a problem of small, medium, and large business alike and in fact of the economy as a whole. One of the cures for this country's economic problems, we are told, is increased productivity.

Production systems, as we have seen, have many different inputs and outputs measured in terms of different units such as manhours, machine hours, units of product, dollars and so on. These inputs and outputs generate costs and revenues. In terms of the three factors which comprise a production system, the first two (the inputs and the work process) generate costs while the third factor (the outputs) generates revenue. Profits are maximized by minimizing costs and maximizing revenues. Since our objective is profit maximization, we will adopt the simplest and probably most common measure of business effectiveness—dollars of profit.

PROBLEMS OF MAXIMIZING PROFIT

When a business appears to be running well and showing a reasonable profit it is difficult for the owner or manager to consider that it still might not be doing as well as it should. If the profit and loss statement shows a profit, how can you tell whether it is the maximum profit that could have been realized? Obviously, you can't by simply looking at the profit and loss statement. The only way to make such a determination is to examine each of the functional areas which affect profit and determine whether they are operating at maximum efficiency. There are no magic formulas for accomplishing this. There are however certain problem areas which are most frequently responsible for profit erosion because of inefficient operating procedures and poor decision making. Each of these must be examined and the proper corrective action taken when necessary. However, it is not sufficient to simply examine operations in these problem areas. One must know what to look for and also how to correct the inefficiencies when they exist.

A major problem in optimizing the operation of a function, as we have previously stated, is that of conflicting objectives. We have mentioned the conflicts that often occur between functional objectives and the overall objectives of the enterprise. However, there can also be conflicting objectives in the performance of a single function. The example of quantity discounts is fairly typical. A vendor offers a substantial discount if large quantities are purchased in a single order at one time. This appears desirable to the purchaser since it reduces the unit cost of the material purchased. However, carrying a large inventory also entails a cost and this cost increases if additional space must be acquired to accomodate the larger orders. Here we have conflicting objectives. One objective is to reduce the cost of the goods purchased; the other is to minimize carrying and warehousing costs. The resolution of this type of problem is not simple because both time and the demand for the material, which may be uncertain, are factors in determining the relationship between the two types of costs.

As another example, consider the establishment and maintenance of quality standards. Most people in and out of business would probably agree that a business should supply goods or services of high quality. In the long run, poor quality entails higher costs for everyone including the supplier of the good or service. However, there are also costs associated with maintaining or improving quality. Every business must establish and then maintain quality standards appropriate for that business and its clientele. The conflict arises between the objectives of achieving the highest quality possible under the circumstances while at the same time minimizing the costs associated with the process.

Still another typical problem is one of resource allocation. Resources are frequently scarce and are always limited. These include human, material and capital resources. Consequently the resources that are available must be allocated to revenue-producing activities in such a way as to maximize the return. However, there are always conflicting demands for resources, and achieving the optimal allocation can often mean the difference between profit and loss for the operation. Furthermore, the greater the number of demands on the resources, the more difficult their optimal allocation becomes.

The problems involving conflicting demands and conflicting objectives occur in certain functional areas more than in others. The resolution of these conflicts is accomplished by using certain analytical techniques that result in a least cost and most effective operating strategy. The application of these techniques in each of the problem areas will produce optimal operating efficiency in each area and lead to overall profit maximization. Of course, it is first necessary to identify what and where the major problem areas are and then describe and explain the tools and techniques that can be applied.

Before identifying problem areas and describing these tools and techniques it may be advisable to discuss what is not included here as part of a profit maximization program. There are areas in most businesses where profits might be increased simply by the application of more resources. Sales or marketing provides a good example. By increasing advertising expenditures, hiring more sales persons, sending sales personnel to sales training programs, and so on, increased sales can and should result. And, of course, other factors remaining the same, an increase in sales should produce an increase in profits. However, increasing profits is not the same as maximizing profits. Maximizing profits implies increasing efficiency, that is, increasing profits *without* increasing the commitment of resources. We will limit our discussion to this type of problem.

PROBLEM AREAS FOR PROFIT MAXIMIZATION

A useful approach to the discussion of business problems is one of classification, that is, to attempt to classify particular groups of problems according to their nature and similarities. With such a classification, solutions can be provided for each class of problem that can be identified. We will attempt to make such a classification and address ourselves to the solution of problems in each class while recognizing that some problems overlap classifications.

Capacity Planning

The long range expectations and eventual performance of a business can be expressed to a large extent by its capacity plans. This is true whether we are considering a single retail store or a manufacturing operation. It is in connection with the capacity plan that market trends in terms of size and location must be considered. Of course, long-range forecasts of demand are difficult and frequently inaccurate. Nevertheless it is the demand for the product or service over the long run that most affects the capacity plan of the business. Too little capacity results in lost revenues while too much means unnecessary and excessive costs. The problem of determining and planning for capacity is crucial to profit maximization.

Inventory Control

Inventories are stocks of goods or supplies which are maintained in the plant either for sale or for use. Inventory must be recorded and accounted for since it represents a substantial capital investment. It also must be replenished when depleted, at optimal times and in optimal quantities. When optimal inventory control procedures are not used, excessive costs occur through overstocks and obsolescence or because of shortages or both. The inventory area is one of the primary sources of profit erosion in most businesses.

Purchasing

Purchasing provides the goods and materials necessary for the operation of the business in the proper quantities, at the proper time and place, and at the lowest cost consistent with established quality standards. The transportation, delivery and to some extent the storage of the purchased goods is also part of this function. To a degree, purchasing and inventory problems overlap. Poor purchasing decisions, delivery delays and so on add to the cost of doing business and consequently reduce profit.

Resource Allocation and Scheduling

The optimal allocation of material, human and capital resources and their phasing or scheduling in the process is a major problem area because it is probably the most difficult function to optimize. Limited resources must always be allocated to produce the maximum revenue. Scheduling problems result in delays, idle time and production bottlenecks all of which can be extremely costly.

Quality Assurance

Quality assurance is the function which establishes quality standards and then assures that those standards are maintained. Quality standards apply to both goods and services, and poor quality of either results in excessive costs due to customer ill will and lost business as well as wasted time, effort and material. On the other hand, the establishment of quality standards at an unrealistically or unnecessarily high level also leads to excessive and unnecessary costs. Determining what the appropriate quality standards are and then maintaining them is a major problem area in business.

Production Control

Primarily applicable to manufacturing operations, the concept of production control can also be applied to nonmanufacturing or service operations of a complex nature. The different operations in any process must be determined and the proper sequence established. Instructions and information necessary for the performance of these operations must be available where and when required. When demand is uneven, decisions regarding overtime, storage, and employment stabilization must be made. This complex of interrelated factors which together determine the structure of the production system must be resolved in a way that most effectively accomplishes the overall objectives of the business. Problems in the production control area and those in resource allocation and scheduling frequently overlap.

Human Resource Management

The greatest contributors to business costs and also to profits are its human resources. This is particularly true in service operations. However, the effective management of these human resources is probably the most difficult task of management. This area has also become one of the most critical in terms of profit maximization. In order to manage human resources effectively, realistic standards of performance are required and employee evaluations are necessary.

The question of how much output is reasonable and should be expected is relatively easy to answer with respect to machines. It is much more difficult to answer with respect to human beings. Nevertheless, because labor represents such a large proportion of the total cost in any business, job and performance evaluation, work measurement, and job design are very important components of an effective production system.

TOOLS AND TECHNIQUES FOR PROFIT MAXIMIZATION

Within each of the problem areas mentioned above, specific tools and techniques for optimizing some function or functions will be discussed in subsequent chapters. However, there are certain more general tools and techniques that can be applied to several different problem areas or that have analytical value in themselves in terms of optimizing operations and maximizing profits. Because of their usefulness, these will be discussed separately.

Cost, Volume, and Breakeven Analysis

Before any problem can be solved, it must first be identified and located. Consequently, the first step in any program of profit maximization is to determine what and where the problems are. Cost, volume, and breakeven analysis is one approach.

Profit has been defined as the difference between total costs and total revenues. Revenues are related to output while costs tend to be input related. Many operations in business contribute to costs without directly influencing revenues. If such costs can be reduced and the level of revenues maintained, profit increases. The study of revenues and costs in relation to output and their effect on profits is called *breakeven analysis*. Breakeven analysis describes the relationship among the factors contributing to costs and revenue at different levels of output. Consequently the analysis provides a concise picture of the operating characteristics of the enterprise under varying circumstances and conditions. It also assists the manager in making decisions regarding optimal operating levels.

Budgets and Cost Control

It is impossible to control costs without knowing exactly what those costs are and what they should be. Consequently, the control of costs has two aspects: a set of realistic cost standards and accurate cost information. One of the most effective tools for establishing and maintaining cost standards is the budget and the budgeting process. Realistic budgets in conjunction with current and accurate cost information are one of the most effective tools of profit maximization.

Forecasting

Capacity planning, inventory control, production scheduling, purchasing and other functions all require some prediction of demand in order for optimal decisions to be made. Consequently, one of the most important techniques applicable to many problem areas is forecasting. There are several forecasting methods that range from the very simple to the extremely complex, and they have various degrees of effectiveness. The selection and description of the most effective of these and their application to the profit maximization problem will be discussed in detail.

Computers and Data Processing

One of the most significant occurrences in business in recent years has been the increased availability of digital computers at costs that are low enough for practically any business to afford. The primary ingredient of all the techniques for profit maximization is current and accurate information. Decisions based on outdated or inaccurate data can only be poor decisions. Management information systems based on the electronic digital computer can provide the type of current and accurate information that is needed. We will discuss the computer and the computer based information system and their application to business problems in general and particularly those applications which are related to the profit maximization problem.

THE PROFIT MAXIMIZATION STRATEGY

Having outlined and briefly discussed the major problem areas as well as some of the tools and techniques available for solving the problems, we will now suggest a strategy for achieving the profit maximization goal both in practice and in print. The following chapters begin with a general discussion and certain preliminaries and then go into a detailed discussion of breakeven analysis. In practice, this analysis should be the first tool utilized and constitutes the first stage in the profit maximization strategy. The first step in achieving any goal is to determine your present position. Breakeven analysis, in providing a picture of the operating characteristics of the business, does exactly that. We will then discuss each of the problem areas in detail beginning with capacity problems and ending with human resource management. In each of these areas we will identify the specific problems which lead to profit erosion and provide solutions. Interspersed where needed will be chapters devoted to the general tools and techniques applicable to several of the problem areas that follow. The final chapter is devoted to the most versatile tool of all, the computer based management information system.

An owner, manager or executive attempting to achieve profit maximization in his own business should follow the sequence provided in these chapters and apply these techniques step by step and chapter by chapter. An analogy can be made between the sequential application of the profit maximization techniques described here to the major problem areas in a business and the plugging of leaks in the hull of a small boat. As each business function is optimized, a profit leak is plugged. By the time the entire sequence is completed, the boat should be free of leaks and the goal of profit maximization should be realized.

2. Beginning a Profit Maximization Program

It seems that getting started is always the hardest part of any new project. This is true whether we are talking about a reducing diet, an exercise program, a program to stop smoking or any other change in a well-established routine. A great deal of inertia must first be overcome, and just as with any other kind of program that represents such a change, a need must exist and be recognized.

The need to begin a profit maximization program is not always as obvious and recognizable as many other conditions that require change. The position of a pointer on a scale clearly indicates that a weight reduction program is in order. A high blood pressure report from a physician signals a need for a change in living habits. But what is a clear indication of the need for a profit maximization program? For a small corporation, two or three years of declining earnings might be such a signal. For a proprietorship or partnership, a single losing year might be the indicator. However, by the time those signals are received, it might very well be too late to initiate the improvement program.

Besides, a business doesn't have to be on the verge of bankruptcy to benefit from profit maximization. Even a well-managed, profitable enterprise may not be operating at peak efficiency and could be experiencing a significant erosion of profits. And why should profits or potential profits be allowed to run down the drain when with some effort and the application of a few of the simple techniques described here they could be recovered and put to good use?

The prudent manager* should always be looking for ways to improve the operations that are within his area of responsibility. This is simply one of the functions of management. There are usually many indicators of less than optimal conditions that the qualified manager, if he is on his toes, cannot avoid seeing: an excessive number of complaints about some aspect of the service provided or about the product; obsolete or slow moving merchandise that must be sold at a loss or at a discount to make room for a new line or model; delays in the delivery or receipt of goods or raw material. These are of course just a few obvious examples. The list of danger signals indicating profit erosion could probably cover several pages. But even without such obvious signals, the manager should still devote a significant portion of his time and effort to looking for ways in which operations could be improved. Most managers do this informally and sometimes intuitively, but in order to be effective and consistent and to be sure that nothing is overlooked, some formal objective procedure should be utilized. A simple and convenient tool for accomplishing this is the checklist.

Checklists serve many purposes. The pilot of a commercial airliner reviews a checklist while preparing for takeoff in order to be sure that he hasn't overlooked any condition that might be detrimental to the safety of his plane or its passengers. A missile control officer goes through a checklist, called a countdown, before every launch for similar reasons. A manager should prepare a checklist to assist him in locating the possible sources of profit erosion in the areas for which he has responsibility. An abbreviated example of a very general checklist is provided in Figure 2.1 in the form of a matrix. The two left-hand columns constitute the checklist itself. The remaining columns are headed by the functional areas, covered in succeeding chapters, in which the causes of the danger signals listed in the first column are likely to occur. The manager can go down the list of signals in column 2 checking off those that are appropriate and then refer to the matrix to determine where to look for the causes.

Of course, this checklist is not applicable for every manager in every

---

*For convenience, the term *manager* will be used here to include entrepreneurs of, or partners in, small businesses. In general, anyone with decision-making responsibility over all or part of an enterprise is a manager.

	Check	Fore-casting	Capacity Planning	Materials Planning	Inventory Control	Pur-chasing	Production Planning & Scheduling	Quality Control	Cost & Budgetary Control	Human Resources	Information Systems
Absenteeism — excessive	✓									X	
Budget overruns	✓								X		X
Customer complaints — product	✓							X			
Customer complaints — delivery	✓				X		X				
Customer complaints — personnel	✓									X	
Failure to take discounts on payables	✓								X		X
Failure to take quantity discounts — purchases	✓				X	X					
Idle capacity	✓	X	X				X				
Idle time	✓						X			X	
Inaccurate or out-of-date information	✓										X
Lack of capacity	✓	X	X				X				
Late deliveries from vendors	✓	X				X					
Low or declining productivity	✓									X	
Obsolete or out-of-date product	✓	X			X		X				
Overtime — excessive	✓	X	X								
Personnel shortages	✓	X	X								
Poor internal communication	✓									X	X
Poor workmanship	✓							X		X	
Product outages	✓				X	X					
Production delays and bottlenecks	✓		X	X	X		X				
Raw material outages or shortages	✓			X	X	X					
Tardiness — excessive	✓									X	

Figure 2.1. Problem checklist and matrix.

line of business. It is simply an example that might be useful for some managers in some types of business with some revisions, deletions, or additions. Each manager should prepare his own checklist tailored to the environment within which he operates. The checklist does not solve the problems. It simply helps to locate them. Nevertheless, and in spite of its simplicity, it is a very useful tool and the starting point for any profit maximization program.

The list of problems or signals in the extreme left-hand column of figure 2.1 are not arranged in order of importance nor are they grouped or categorized in any way. The individual manager going over this list might immediately eliminate many of these signals as not being pertinent to his own operation. On the other hand, they might suggest other signals or problems that are appropriate and lead to a greatly expanded checklist. Because of their generality, some discussion of these problems might be useful at this point.

Budget Overruns

The budget is the basic tool for controlling costs and expenditures. Exceeding budgeted amounts can be due to two factors: either the budgeting and cost control processes are unrealistic or inaccurate, or other factors within the organization have gone out of control and the results are reflected in the cost information. Any budget overrun should be taken by the manager as a warning. When it occurs he should first check the assumptions that went into the preparation of the budget, then the accuracy of the information itself, and finally, if those items check out, continue down the checklist for other warning signals which are certain to be there.

Customer Complaints

The primary function of any business organization is to serve some market. The market consists of customers and potential customers. The market in fact is one of the major constituencies of the business. When this constituency is dissatisfied for any reason the business is in trouble. The primary indication of dissatisfaction is complaints. It is important for every business organization to have some mechanisms not only for handling customer complaints, but also for recording them. No business organization is perfect. There will always be cases of defective merchandise or product, late delivery, discourteous personnel, and so on. However, any increase in the number of complaints should be called to the attention of the manager since that may indicate a serious problem. Depending upon the nature of the complaint, the manager can determine which functional area—quality control, production control, personnel, etc.—should be investigated.

Absenteeism and Tardiness

Since labor costs have become the major cost of doing business, excessive absenteeism and tardiness can be a major contributor to profit erosion. In addition to the direct costs associated with these factors and their effect on the production system, they may also indicate a serious flaw in the human resource or personnel system, and reflect serious dissatisfaction with jobs, working conditions, rates of pay, management, and so on.

Excessive Overtime, Unused or Lack of Capacity, Idle Time or Personnel Shortages

These five factors, which are prime manifestations of profit erosion, are grouped together because they often result from the same or similar causes, that is, poor planning. Excessive overtime means premium pay for work that ordinarily would be performed at straight-time rates. Overtime may be related to the lack of physical capacity or to personnel shortages. Just as costly to the business is excessive capacity and idle time. In these cases, costs are incurred for non-productivity. When these situations occur, the underlying causes may be found in several different functional areas such as faulty or poor procedures, poor capacity and production planning, and of course the human resource area.

Low or Declining Productivity

Productivity is of course related to several different factors. The first that comes to mind is the human resource factor. When productivity is down or declining it is natural to examine the personnel system first to determine if changes have occurred in the hiring or training process or if reasons for job dissatisfaction exist. However, productivity is also dependent on several other factors such as planning and inventory and purchasing procedures. Shortages and production bottlenecks can affect productivity just as seriously as personnel problems.

Obsolete or Out-of-Date Products

Inventories of obsolete or out-of-date products result in excessive costs. The root cause of this condition is generally poor forecasting. However, less than optimal inventory procedures can also produce this result. Whenever it becomes necessary to discount or reduce prices in order to move merchandise, profit erosion occurs. The remedy often lies in those two functional areas, that is, forecasting and inventory control.

Product and Raw Material Outages or Shortages

Shortages and outages affect costs through production delays, idle time, idle capacity, late deliveries to customers and so on. The causes generally lie in the purchasing and inventory areas with respect to the end product, and in these same areas plus materials planning with respect to raw materials. In either case, end product or raw material, shortages and outages result in profit erosion.

Failure to Take Appropriate Discounts

Discounts for quantity purchases and timely payment represent significant savings. Conversely, failure to take such discounts result in excessive costs and erosion of profits. In the case of payables, the functional areas that are likley to be at fault are cost control and information processing. With respect to purchase discounts, the functional areas involved are purchasing and inventory control.

Poor Workmanship

Poor workmanship leads to waste. Waste of time and waste of material since both time and additional material must be spent in correcting defects and errors. When poor workmanship goes uncorrected, customer dissatisfaction results with the possible loss of business. In both cases, profits or potential profits are lost. The places to look for the causes of poor workmanship are in the human resource system primarily, and secondarily in the quality system.

Lack of Internal Communication and Inaccurate or Out-of-Date Information

In today's fast moving and competitive economy, timely and accurate information is essential for effective management. When one part of the organization doesn't know what the other part is doing (marketing and manufacturing, for example) or when managerial decisions are based on inaccurate or out-of-date information, the results can be disastrous. An effective management information system has become an essential part of every business organization regardless of size. Indications of poor information for decision making require investigation into the MIS.

Production Bottlenecks

Production bottlenecks or delays of any kind are costly. The obvious functional areas that could be at fault are production planning, scheduling and control. However, other functional areas that contribute to bottlenecks include inventory control, and materials and capacity planning. Problems in these areas can often be traced to poor forecasting.

Late Deliveries from Vendors

Late deliveries of product and raw materials from vendors contribute to production delays, idle time, idle capacity and so on. When deliveries are consistently late, the purchasing function is most likely at fault and must bear the responsibility. The topic of efficient purchasing is covered in Chapter 8.

It should be apparent to the reader at this point that many categories of problems overlap and also that the sources or causes of these problems can often be traced to more than one functional area. When a production bottleneck occurs we also have idle time and idle capacity. In cases of poor workmanship we may also have low or declining productivity as well as signals of customer dissatisfaction. Turning to the functional areas, forecasting affects all planning activities, the human resource area has an effect on practically everything else, and so on. As a result of these overlaps and interdependencies, redundancies do occur in a checklist and matrix such as Figure 2.1. However, redundancies are preferable to oversights. With redundancies, everything gets checked out at least once.

The checklist is probably the simplest diagnostic tool that is available to management. Yet it is surprising how infrequently it is used in any formal way in business. Of course, most managers do use mental checklists informally, often without even realizing that they are using one. However, unless the checklist is an actual physical document used periodically as part of a formal review procedure, too many items are forgotten or simply ignored and various manifestations of profit erosion tend to be overlooked until the problems become so serious that they force themselves upon the attention of management. However, by the time that happens they may already be past solution or if not have already cost the organization significantly.

The profit maximization program must begin with the realization that any business organization, profitable or not, may not be operating at maximum efficiency. Problems and inefficiencies do exist, and once that fact is recognized, the next step is to identify them and locate their causes. Determining and implementing the remedies constitutes the subject of the following chapters.

One last remark on the management of small and medium-sized businesses. The effective manager is an efficient delegator. Competent, ambitious, knowledgeable and well-trained subordinates are essential to the successful operation of a business regardless of its size. No individual, no matter how competent, can know everything and do everything that has to be done to operate a business optimally. An obvious exception to this remark would be the one-person business, a class of enterprise which is declining in numbers for one of two reasons. Either the inefficiencies in this type of business are so great that it fails to survive, or success leads to growth in which case it is no longer a one-person business.

The point of the previous paragraph is not to attempt to define a good or effective size for any business but simply to emphasize that the manager who devotes all his time to the day-to-day operations has no time to manage. And without time to manage, profit erosion will go uncorrected and probably unnoticed until it is too late.

3. Business Functions and Organizations

The techniques and concepts presented in the chapters that follow will in some cases require a considerable amount of concentration on the part of the reader. Many of these are quite simple. Some, though complicated in their conception, have been simplified for easy, or relatively easy, application to the profit maximization problems of small and medium-sized businesses. The ones that the reader will no doubt find the most troublesome are those that are inherently quantitative in nature. Nevertheless, even those will require no knowledge of advanced or even difficult mathematics. The most required of the reader is a reasonable facility with the basic arithmetic operations, some simple algebraic manipulations, and the ability to reason logically. In most cases, even that much mathematics is required only for understanding the rationale underlying the techniques. Actual calculations are easily provided by computer programs which for the most part are available as software packages provided by the computer manufacturer.

In order to illustrate the application of the various profit maximization techniques covered here, frequent examples will be provided. The examples will be as realistic as possible without becoming overly complicated and will show how the solution to the problem can be obtained. The reader should understand that each example represents a compromise between realism and simplicity. If the example is too complicated, the principle or technique being illustrated may be lost in the intricacies. On the other hand, if the situation is oversimplified, it may bear little or no relationship to the real and practical problems with which the manager must contend.

BUSINESS TYPES, FUNCTIONS, AND ORGANIZATIONS

The number of different types of businesses and their organization is so great, even in the small and medium-sized categories, that it would be impossible to provide examples representative of all of them. However, although all the problems, and the techniques for their solution, that are presented here are not necessarily applicable to all types of businesses, it is surprising how often different types of organizations experience the same or similar kinds of problems. Again, even though all business types do not perform all the same functions within the organization, there are certain functions common to all.

Every business, and we assume that the term *business* is synonymous with profit-seeking enterprise, is involved in the two basic functions of buying and selling. For the term *buying* we could substitute the word *acquiring* or even more appropriate, *purchasing*. For selling, the appropriate term is *marketing*. These functions are performed in every type of business whether it is involved in manufacturing, the retail sales of a finished product or the provision of a service. In retailing, the product sold must be purchased from a manufacturer or wholesaler. In manufacturing, purchasing involves raw material, component parts, equipment and so on. Even for the service business, the skills, materials or equipment necessary to provide the service must first be acquired or purchased. And of course in order to realize a profit, the product or service must be marketed.

Since both buying and selling involve financial transactions, an accounting function is required to keep track of those transactions and to let management know the condition of the enterprise at any point in time. Closely associated with the accounting function but frequently treated separately is the function of information processing. And finally, since one of the major resources of any business enterprise is its personnel, all are concerned to some extent with the management of human resources.

In summary then, the five functions common to all businesses regardless of type are:

1. Marketing
2. Purchasing
3. Accounting
4. Information processing
5. Human resource management

The commonality of these five functions to all businesses does not mean that every business regardless of size or type has formal departments coinciding with each of the functions. Some of these functions are performed by formal departments within an enterprise while some may be performed on an informal basis or as part of another functional department. In the one person business, for example, all functions must be performed by the same individual with no formal departmentalization whatsoever. In fact, to talk of formal departments in that case would be nonsense.

As a business grows in terms of volume, personnel, and so on increasing departmentalization occurs. In a small business, information processing is frequently merged with the accounting function. In a larger business, it usually becomes a separate functional department. However, no matter what type or size of business, these five functions must be performed either formally or informally. It must be mentioned that the relative importance of the five basic functions vary among different types of businesses. In some, marketing is considered to be of much greater importance than purchasing. In others, department stores, for example, purchasing is at least as important as marketing. In fact, department store department managers are usually called buyers, not sales managers.

Of course many other functions are performed, and these may be departmentalized depending upon the type, size and degree of specialization considered desirable for the business. Some of these are:

1. Manufacturing
2. Engineering
3. Warehousing and shipping
4. Production control
5. Quality control
6. Financing

And many of these functions are further broken down into subfunctions which may also be departmentalized. For example, marketing may be divided into sales, advertising, and promotion; or manufacturing, into fabrication and assembly. The profit maximization techniques that are covered in the following chapters apply to these various functional areas whether, in a particular business, they are recognized formally or performed informally, departmentalized or not.

For the convenience of the reader, we will describe three different types of business organizations which will be referred to in some of the examples provided in subsequent chapters. By using the same business organizations in a variety of situations, a certain continuity will be maintained and the reader will not have to familiarize himself with the details and characteristics of a new business organization every time a new illustration is presented. The three organizations that will be described below represent a manufacturing business, a retailer and a service business.

Westwind, Inc.

Westwind, Inc. is a medium-sized manufacturer whose main plant and corporate headquarters is located in Los Angeles, California. Westwind has two major product lines: ventilating fans and room air conditioners. These products are manufactured in various models in the Los Angeles plant and marketed through electrical supply houses in the western United States. Westwind maintains sales offices in Seattle, Washington; Houston, Texas; Denver, Colorado; and St. Louis, Missouri; and warehouses in Seattle and Houston. The basic organization of Westwind is shown in Figure 3.1.

The Butler Shoe Company

The Butler Shoe Company is a family owned business started by George Butler in 1948. The company operates three stores, the original store located downtown, and two stores in suburban shopping malls. George Butler retired from active participation in the business in 1977 and management has been in the hands of Stephen, his oldest son, since that time. The stores handle several lines of women's and children's shoes, an expensive and a modestly priced line of men's shoes, and a complete line of athletic shoes for both men and women. Stephen Butler is president and general manager of the company. A manager for each store reports directly to the president. Each manager is responsible for store operation and personnel. Merchandise is ordered through a central purchasing department but is delivered directly to each store. A full-time accountant reports directly to the president. A simple organization chart for the company is shown in Figure 3.2.

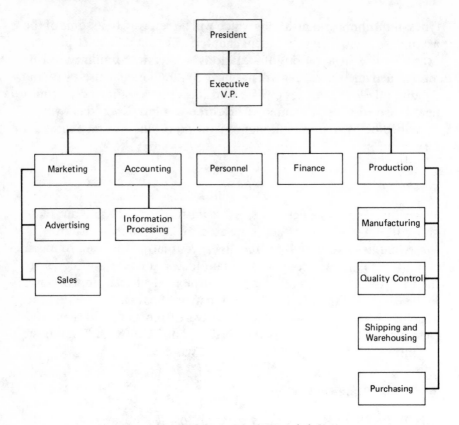

Figure 3.1. Organization chart: Westwind, Inc.

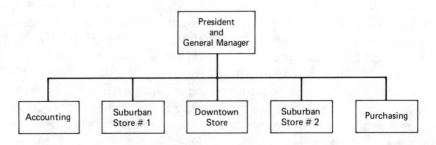

Figure 3.2. Organization chart: Butler Shoe Company

Tech-Ed Schools, Inc.

Tech-Ed began as a proprietary business school in Philadelphia approximately fifteen years ago. In the beginning, the school taught secretarial and office skills such as typing, shorthand, bookkeeping, filing, etc., exclusively. However, with the advent and popularity of electronic computers in business, the school branched out and added courses in data processing, computer programming, computerized accounting systems and word processing. In 1979 Tech-Ed made its third move into larger and more modern facilities taking over three floors of a modern office building in downtown Philadelphia.

The president of Tech-Ed is the chief administrative officer. Reporting to him are the academic vice president who is in charge of all phases of the curriculum as well as the academic staff, the financial vice president who is also the controller, and the administrative vice president who has responsibility for facilities and all nonacademic phases of the operation. A basic organization chart for Tech-Ed is provided in Figure 3.3.

By referring to Westwind, the Butler Shoe Company, and Tech-Ed in subsequent chapters, we can show how the various profit maximization techniques apply to manufacturing organizations, retailers and service businesses. From time to time, where appropriate, ex-

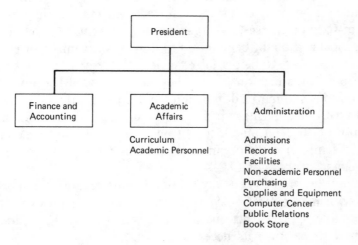

Figure 3.3. Organization chart: Tech-Ed Schools, Inc.

amples featuring other types of businesses will also be used as illustrations.

ORGANIZATION FOR PROFIT MAXIMIZATION

In a one-man business, there is obviously no organizational structure. The owner-manager performs all of the functions that are necessary and divides his time among these functions as circumstances require. However, as soon as the owner-manager hires a second person to assist him, some organization is required. Responsibilities for performance of the various functions must be divided and some delegation of authority becomes necessary. As the business grows, the need for some formal organizational structure becomes apparent if only to avoid duplication of effort in some cases, or lack of responsibility for certain functions in others and overlapping and, therefore, conflicting authority.

An organization is simply a group of individuals, each having specified duties and responsibilities, banded together for the purpose of accomplishing some common goal. In a business organization, the primary goal is realizing a profit and, in the context of this book, maximizing profits.

There is of course no single correct organizational structure for all types of businesses. In fact, there is no single correct organizational structure for any single business. However, in most small and even medium-sized businesses, the organization just seems to grow without any particular thought being given to how it is organized or even to whether it appears to be organized efficiently. Profits can be eroded due to poor organization just as they can be eroded for any of the other reasons summarized in chapter 1. Consequently, when beginning a profit maximization program, the manager should look at his organization to determine if it is structured to achieve the common goal efficiently or if the organization itself might actually hinder the achievement of that goal.

The quickest and easiest way to examine the organizational structure is with an organization chart. If one does not already exist, it is a simple matter to construct one which depicts the way the business is organized to perform its necessary functions. Organization charts serve a useful purpose in disclosing defects in the assignment of duties and responsibilities. Often, when a business which simply grew without attempting to develop a formal organizational structure constructs such a chart, deficiencies in the organization can be detected. Functions and activities may not be logically arranged or situated. Some functions may have been split with a part of the function assigned to one department and another part to another. Duplication of work assignments may have been made with the result that two or more departments are performing the same tasks. Unrelated activities may be grouped together, and specialized departments may have been assigned duties which they are not qualified to perform properly. Some departments become overdeveloped in relation to the others, with subsequent waste of money and effort on unprofitable activities. At various levels in the organization, the number of persons reporting to one supervisor may exceed the number that can be effectively supervised. The undesirable features in an organization may continue indefinitely unless a chart brings them into focus.

There is of course no single "right" type of organization. This has been stated previously but warrants repeating. There are however some principles of organization that should be adhered to. We'll discuss some of these organizational principles before getting into the more technical aspects of profit maximization.

Certain principles of organization appear to be generally accepted, no doubt due to the fact that in their application the results tend to verify their correctness. In analyzing the organizational structure of the firm, the manager should keep these principles in mind:

1. The organization should be structured so that every part contributes to the attainment of its objective. Every department, section and key individual should be evaluated on the basis of how well it or they contribute to the organizational goal.
2. In every business organization the authority for every decision must rest some place and the seat of that authority must be specified. This includes the ultimate authority for all decisions and consequently for the performance of the organization itself. Furthermore, the lines of authority from the manager to every subordinate must be clearly drawn.
3. There is a limit to the number of subordinates that any individual can manage effectively. That number may vary depending on the capabilities of the manager and the complexity of the function or functions managed. Nevertheless, a limit does exist

and its determination in the light of the various factors which influence it is important for every managerial position in the organization.

4. At every level in the organization the authority should exist for making decisions appropriate at that level. Only decisions that cannot be made at a given level should be referred upward to a higher level.

5. Authority can and should be delegated but responsibility is absolute. No superior can relinquish responsibility for authorized actions of his subordinates. However, responsibility for actions taken under delegated authority cannot be greater than that implied by the authority delegated.

6. No subordinate should have more than one superior. When this principle is violated, it leads to divided loyalties and split responsibilities and interferes with efficient performance.

7. All activities performed by the organization should be divided and grouped in a way that contributes most efficiently and effectively to the achievement of the organization's objectives.

8. The authority, responsibility, function and content of every position must be clearly defined. This will avoid overlapping responsibilities, duplication of effort, and conflict among managers, supervisors, and employees.

9. Because conditions change continuously, provisions for change must be available. No organization or organization chart can be absolutely fixed and rigid. The organization that becomes inflexible will be unable to adjust to technical, economic, and social changes in the environment and is doomed to eventual failure.

Constructing an organization chart and evaluating the organizational structure in the light of the nine principles discussed above is a vital preliminary step in the profit maximization program. An unwieldy and inefficient organization cannot possibly achieve its profit potential regardless of the sophisticated tools applied and methods used, that is, until the inefficiencies in the structure itself are eliminated. When the organization is spare and efficient, you are ready for a profit maximization program.

4. Cost, Profit and Breakeven Analysis

In Chapter 1 we briefly discussed several of the most crucial problem areas involved in profit maximization. We began with capacity planning and continued through human resource management. The areas and topics covered correspond roughly with Chapters 6 through 12 of this book. However, in the first chapter we also identified several tools or techniques for profit maximization which apply or have an effect on several of the problem areas. The first of these tools is *cost, profit and breakeven analysis*. This technique is extremely useful in answering such questions as how much should I produce, or at what level should I operate? It is also helpful in making decisions regarding investments in plant or equipment and prices. In general, the analysis provides the manager with a concise picture of the operating characteristics of the firm and the relationships among revenues, costs, profits, and operating levels. Because of its importance to the understanding of these relationships and its overall usefulness to the manager, we begin our discussion of profit maximization with this topic.

Any production system consists of a set of inputs, the process itself and a set of outputs. It is the process that transforms the inputs into the desired set of outputs. In the planning of any business venture, specifying the desired outputs is usually the initial step since the outputs generate revenue. In order for the business to be profitable, the outputs must have greater value in the marketplace than the combined values of the inputs and the investment in the process. In fact, the total should actually be greater than the sum of its parts in this instance. Only then can the enterprise be profitable.

In this analysis of the operating characteristics of the firm it is useful to move from the input-process-output concept to a cost-revenue concept, or to be even more precise, to a fixed-cost–variable-cost–revenue concept. Let's consider each of these factors separately before putting them together into a picture of the operating characteristics of the firm called a *breakeven chart*.

Revenue is another word for income. It is a function of the output delivered to the market. Total revenue in monetary terms is equal to the quantity sold times the price charged per unit. If the output of the firm consists of more than a single product or service, the total revenue is simply the sum of the revenues generated by each. Revenue is associated with output.

Fixed costs are those costs that are not directly related to the volume of production. Consequently, fixed costs are constant regardless of the level of output. The fixed costs are generally process costs. They are the costs associated with the production elements that make up the process factor of the production system. Examples of fixed cost elements include:

1. Depreciation on plant and equipment
2. Salaries of nonproduction workers (managers, supervisors, office staff, etc.)
3. Taxes and insurance
4. Interest on investment
5. Utilities

Fixed costs result from investment in the production process. When they are depreciable, they are depreciated as a function of time, not as a function of production quantity or value.

Variable costs, often referred to as direct costs, are related to the system inputs. These costs are incurred on a per unit of production basis and are computed by multiplying the variable cost per unit by the number of units produced. Direct labor and direct materials are typical variable costs since they can be charged directly to each unit of production. Management's primary method of control over the production system is exercised by the scheduling of inputs to the process thus incurring direct or variable costs. In the short run, management has no control over the fixed costs.

The concept of the short and long run is a convenient device for categorizing time periods for planning purposes. These are not fixed periods of time. The long run is a period long enough so that all of the process factors can be adjusted. Plant capacity can be added or disposed of, equipment can be purchased or discarded, etc. In the long run, all costs are variable. In the short run, the process factors cannot be changed. Consequently, management must exercise control by varying the input factors. It is only in the short run that we can differentiate between fixed and variable costs.

Time periods corresponding to the short and long run vary depending upon the type of business being considered. A business that requires a very large investment in plant and equipment, such as a manufacturer of durable goods, would define the short run as constituting a much longer time period than would a management consultant, for example, with a very small investment in plant and equipment. The short run for the latter might be determined by the period of the lease he holds on his office space.

Consider Tech-Ed Schools, Inc. the proprietary business and computer school described in the previous chapter. Tech-Ed is of course a service business. The school occupies three floors of a modern office building in downtown Philadelphia. These facilities, consisting of classrooms, a computer center, offices, supply rooms, etc., have been leased for a period of three years and the rent is a fixed cost. It is fixed since the landlord would not reduce the rent if several of the classrooms were unused during a particular semester. Nor would he prorate it on the basis of the number of rooms actually used by the school. Since this cost is constant it is independent of the level of production, in this case measured by the number of student-hours taught. The three year lease is the major determinant of the short run for Tech-Ed.

In distinguishing between other fixed and variable costs, administrative and clerical salaries are of course fixed. However, teaching salaries are not so clear-cut. Some teachers, considered permanent staff, have contracts and their salaries are obligations that must be paid regardless of the number of students or classes that they teach. Therefore, those salaries should be treated as fixed costs. On the other hand, some part-time teachers are hired only to meet the demand for certain courses that cannot be staffed by the full-time teachers. If sufficient students do not register to make it worthwhile to run these courses, they are simply cancelled and the part-time teachers need not be paid. Those salaries can therefore be considered as variable costs. As the previous illustration shows, the distinction between fixed and variable costs is not always clear-cut.

BREAKEVEN

Breakeven is an easy concept to understand. It is not however always easy to determine. Breakeven is the level of operations at which total costs equal total revenue and consequently neither a profit nor a loss is incurred. The breakeven concept is most easily presented with a device known as a *breakeven chart*. The breakeven chart is a convenient tool for managers to use in determining the firm's optimal operating levels under differing circumstances. The chart illustrates the relationships between costs and revenues at different operating levels. A typical breakeven chart is illustrated in Figure 4.1.

In Figure 4.1 the vertical axis of the chart is scaled in dollars. The horizontal axis is scaled in terms of production quantity and can represent either percent of production capacity or units of production. The horizontal line above and parallel to the volume axis is labeled *fixed cost,* which we will abbreviate FC. For the short run period represented by the chart, it is easy to see that the fixed costs remain constant, that is, at the same level regardless of the volume of production. Fixed costs are the same for zero or no production as they are for the maximum level of production shown on the chart.

The line labeled *total cost* (TC) begins at zero production at the point where the fixed cost line meets the vertical axis, and then slants upward to the right. The difference between total costs and fixed costs, (TC − FC) represents the variable costs. The chart illustrates that at zero production there are no variable costs, but as production in-

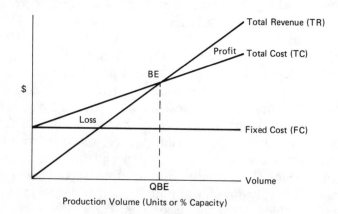

Figure 4.1. Typical breakeven chart.

creases, variable costs also increase in direct proportion to production. This direct or linear relationship between production and variable costs is a simplification that does not always hold. However, it is a reasonable approximation in most instances, and, as we will show later, the chart can be modified when this assumption proves to be unrealistic.

Finally, the *total revenue* line (TR) slants from lower left to upper right beginning at zero production and zero dollars. Total revenue intersects the total cost line at the breakeven point which is labeled BE. The chart illustrates that at breakeven, total costs and total revenue are equal and there is no profit or loss. The dashed vertical line running from the breakeven point to the horizontal axis identifies the level of production at breakeven and is designated QBE.

The difference between total revenue and total cost is either profit or loss depending upon which is greater. When total revenue is less than total cost, the firm is operating at a loss. This is shown in Figure 4.1 to the left of the breakeven point. When total revenue exceeds total cost, a profit is realized. This occurs at production volumes to the right of the breakeven quantity.

ANALYSIS

There are two factors to be considered in the analysis of a breakeven chart: first, the position of the breakeven point in relation to the volume of production, and second, the marginal or additional profit that can be realized for each additional unit that can be produced. The marginal return per unit is called the *contribution margin*. If we let p represent the unit price of the product and v represent the variable cost per unit, then $p - v = CM$, the contribution margin. So long as CM is a positive value, that is the price per unit is greater than the variable cost per unit, then the sale of each additional unit of product (or service) makes a contribution to profit. This contribution margin is represented by the *slope* of the total revenue line in Figure 4.1. The steeper the slope of the TR line, the greater the contribution margin. On the other hand, if we were to rotate the TR line in a clockwise direction so that it became almost parallel to the horizontal axis, then each additional unit produced would contribute very little to profit. The steepness of the TR line is affected by the difference between price and variable cost. If we can make this difference greater, the contribution margin increases and the slope of the TR line gets steeper. This difference can be increased, as any businessman knows, either by decreasing the variable cost per unit or by increasing the price. Variable costs can be decreased by increasing the efficiency of the operation and various methods for accomplishing this are covered in succeeding chapters. However, variable costs are not easy to decrease because direct wages, material costs and so on cannot usually be arbitrarily lowered by management. On the other hand, management can increase the price of the product by managerial decision. Therefore, one way to increase the contribution margin might simply be to increase the price of the product. We will consider that option shortly.

First however let us consider the position of the breakeven point in terms of production volume. It is easy to see from Figure 4.1 that the further to the right we operate in terms of volume, the greater the profit we realize. The limitation on volume is of course the physical capacity of the plant. We cannot exceed 100% of capacity. For the purpose of a breakeven analysis it is assumed, at least initially, that the market will absorb all increases in production up to 100% of capacity. In other words, we assume that we can sell all that we can produce.

Consequently, the simple solution to the volume question appears to be to operate at 100% of capacity all the time. However, we must now reconsider the initial assumption. Is it valid to assume that we can sell all that we can produce? In most cases it is not. In the long run we can adjust our capacity in accordance with the demand for the product. In the short run, we cannot. Therefore, we must be concerned about demand because the demand for our product determines our position on the volume scale.

Although as managers of small and medium-sized businesses we have little effect on the overall market demand for the product, we do have control over one factor that affects the demand for our product vis à vis our competition, and that is the price we set. By raising or lowering our price we can increase or decrease the demand for our product in a competitive market. Raising the price will decrease the demand forcing us to operate at a lower level on the volume scale while decreasing the price should have the opposite effect.

Increasing or decreasing the price while variable costs remain the same increases or decreases the contribution $(p - v)$ and also increases or decreases the slope of the TR line. For example, Figure 4.2

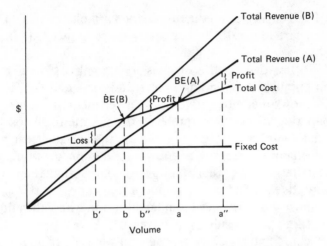

Figure 4.2. Breakeven chart with two pricing policies.

illustrates a breakeven chart that is similar to the one in Figure 4.1 except that it has two total revenue lines. Each TR line corresponds to a
different pricing policy, policy A and policy B, where price B is higher
than price A. It seems obvious, that all else being equal, the higher
price policy has a lower breakeven point in terms of volume and produces greater profits than would the lower price. However, market
and demand factors must be taken into consideration here. If at price
B, the market will demand only quantity b′, then the firm would have
to operate at a loss, and price A, even though requiring a higher
volume to break even, would be more advantageous to the firm than
price B.

Suppose that at price A the market will demand a quantity a″ and at
price B it will demand quantity b″. In that case a profit would be
realized at both price levels. However, the breakeven chart shows that
profit would be higher with price A, and A is therefore the better pricing policy even though it requires a higher breakeven point than B.

As we mentioned earlier, profit can also be increased at a given price
by reducing variable costs. Suppose that in a particular instance we
could reduce variable costs by installing some new and more efficient
production equipment. This would however require an investment
that would add to fixed costs. Let alternative A be to maintain the
status quo and alternative B be to purchase the new equipment leading

to higher fixed costs but a reduction in the variable cost per unit. The breakeven chart illustrating these alternatives is provided in Figure 4.3.

Figure 4.3 has two fixed cost lines, two total cost lines and two breakeven points corresponding to alternatives A and B. The breakeven chart shows that alternative B, the investment in the new equipment is superior to the status quo even though the fixed costs under that alternative are increased. By reducing the variable cost per unit the breakeven point is reached at a lower level of production, point b, and for every level greater than b, profits are larger than they would be under alternative A. The reader should not assume that this is always the case. Figure 4.4 illustrates a similar situation where the additional investment does not result in a lower breakeven point. It is the breakeven chart and its construction and analysis that enables the manager to compare alternative policies and determine which is optimal under the given circumstances.

Breakeven analysis using the breakeven chart is a convenient and simple tool for determining optimal operating levels under specific market conditions. It is also extremely useful for comparing alternative investment and pricing policies. However, the breakeven chart is not the answer to all of the firm's problems and it does have many limitations. For example, the breakeven chart is most useful for analyzing a single product at a single location. When several products

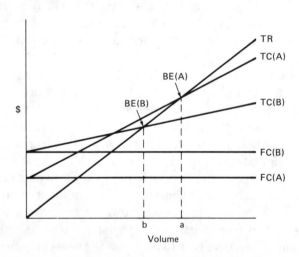

Figure 4.3. Breakeven chart with two investment policies.

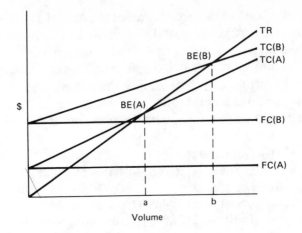

Figure 4.4. Breakeven chart with two investment policies.

are handled by the firm, as is usually the case, a separate chart for each product serves as a means for comparing the operating characteristics of the firm with respect to each. Of course, the fixed cost for each product is that product's prorated share of the total fixed cost. Different plants or locations can also be compared using separate breakeven charts. When an attempt is made to use a single chart to analyze several products, the chart becomes very confusing and difficult to interpret.

Frequently, situations in a multiproduct firm with limited investment dollars or capacity involve decisions regarding product mix. That is, how much of each product is it optimal for us to handle or produce? This is a problem in the optimal allocation of resources, and, while the breakeven chart is useful in displaying the operating characteristics of the firm with regard to each product, it does not provide the solution to that type of problem. There are however other tools that do, and these are discussed later in this book. Some of the types of problems for which the breakeven chart is useful are illustrated in the example which follows.

Westwind, Inc.

One of the best revenue producers in Westwind's product line is their Model 350, 10,000 Btu room air conditioner. Westwind sells about 5000 of these units per year at a price of $220 per unit. The annual fixed costs allocated to the production of the Model 350 are $200,000 and the variable cost per unit is $150. Figure 4.5 is a breakeven chart for the Model 350 and shows that the breakeven point is approximately 2,857 units. With sales of 5000 units, the annual profit is $150,000. The profit or loss is simply the difference between total revenue for the product and total costs where the total costs are the sum of the fixed costs and the variable costs for 5000 units:

$$\begin{aligned}
\text{Fixed costs} &= \$200,000 \\
\text{Variable costs} &= \$750,000 \ (5000 \text{ times } \$150) \\
\text{Total costs} &= \$950,000 \ (\$200,000 + \$750,000) \\
\text{Total revenue} &= \$1,100,000 \ (5000 \text{ times } \$220) \\
\text{Profit} &= \$150,000 \ (\$1,100,000 - \$950,000)
\end{aligned}$$

Westwind's production vice president has proposed the installation of some new production equipment which would raise the fixed costs for the Model 350 to $300,000 per year but which he claims would reduce the variable costs by approximately 10%. That is, variable costs per unit produced would decrease from $150 to $135. Should the new equipment be installed?

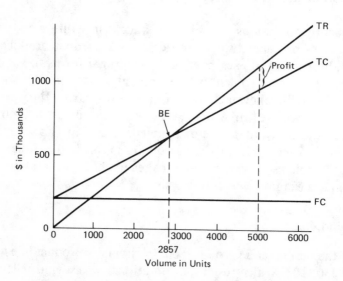

Figure 4.5. Breakeven chart for Westwinds Model 350.

This is the type of problem conveniently solved using the breakeven chart. A new breakeven chart showing the operating characteristics under the new set of conditions, that is, with the installation of the new equipment, is provided in Figure 4.6. Under these circumstances, the breakeven point increases to 3,529 units and the profit on sales of 5000 units declines to $125,000. It is clear that the installation of the new equipment would not be a good investment.

In continuing to make a case for the new equipment, the production vice president suggested that the price of the product should be raised from $220 per unit to $230. He justified the price increase on the basis that the quality and durability of the product would be improved by the new equipment and the process change that would be involved. However, the marketing vice president objected to the price increase estimating that, at the new price, sales would decline by approximately 10% or 500 units. The effects of both the price increase and the installation of the new equipment were analyzed with the breakeven chart in Figure 4.7. With the two changes, the breakeven point becomes 3,158 units but profits on sales of 4500 units are now only $127,500. Consequently, the proposals for both the new equipment and the price increase were rejected.

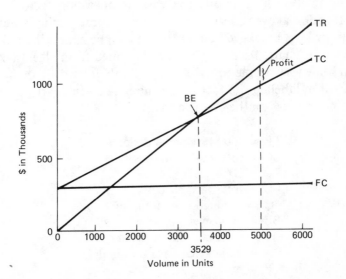

Figure 4.6. Breakeven chart for Westwinds Model 350 with new equipment.

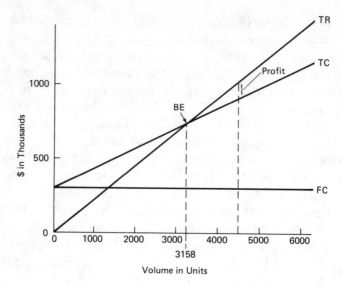

Figure 4.7. Breakeven chart for Westwinds Model 350 with new equipment and price increase.

ALGEBRAIC SOLUTIONS

The breakeven chart is a graphic presentation of a set of simple algebraic relationships among the various operating factors of interest. If the breakeven chart is constructed accurately, the values such as profit or loss, breakeven quantity, etc. can be approximated quite well from the chart. Precise values are obtained from algebraic solutions to some very simple equations. The symbols used are the same as those used in labeling the factors on the breakeven chart plus a few that do not appear on the chart, and are:

$$
\begin{aligned}
TR &= \text{total revenue in dollars} \\
TC &= \text{total cost in dollars} \\
FC &= \text{fixed costs} \\
TVC &= \text{total variable costs} \\
Q &= \text{production quantity or volume} \\
BE &= \text{breakeven point} \\
p &= \text{price per unit in dollars} \\
v &= \text{variable cost per unit in dollars} \\
P &= \text{profit}
\end{aligned}
$$

Total revenue equals the quantity in units multiplied by the price per unit, or TR = Qp. Total cost must equal fixed costs plus total variable costs, or TC = FC + TVC. Total variable costs equal the quantity in units multiplied by the variable cost per unit, or TVC = Qv. Since breakeven is the point at which total cost is equal to total revenue we simply equate the two and then substitute where appropriate an equivalent expression that contains the symbol for the value of interest. For example, if we want the breakeven quantity, we are interested in Q at the breakeven point. Starting with the initial equality, we get:

$$TR = TC$$
$$Qp = FC + TVC$$
$$Qp = FC + Qv$$

Solving for Q we get,

$$Qp - Qv = FC$$
$$Q(p - v) = FC$$
$$Q = \frac{FC}{p - v}$$

For the Westwind situation as depicted in Figure 4.5,

$$FC = \$200,000$$
$$p = \$220 \text{ per unit}$$
$$v = \$150 \text{ per unit}$$
$$Q = \frac{FC}{p - v} = \frac{\$200,000}{\$220 - \$150} = 2,857$$

The previous formula provided the breakeven quantity in units of production. With slight modifications we can find formulas that provide breakeven in dollars and in percent of capacity.

These formulas are respectively:

$$BE (\$) = \frac{FC}{1 - (v/p)}$$

$$BE (\% \text{ capacity}) = \frac{FC}{(p - v)(\text{total capacity in units})} \times 100\%$$

For Westwind:

$$BE\,(\$) = \frac{\$200{,}000}{1 - \$150/\$220} = \$628{,}536$$

Assuming that total capacity for the Model 350 is 6000 units,

$$BE\,(\%\ capacity) = \frac{\$200{,}000}{(\$220 - \$150)\,(6000)} \times 100\% = 47.6\%$$

SOME REFINEMENTS TO THE BREAKEVEN CHART

As the level of operations changes, relationships among the various operating factors may also change. This of course would require that changes be made to the basic breakeven chart. Two common modifications to the chart involve possible changes to the fixed cost line and to the total cost line.

It is not uncommon for variable costs to change as the production quantity increases. This could be the result of the necessity for paying overtime rates in order to increase production. Obviously, an increase in direct labor rates is an increase in the variable costs. Also, as the level of production increases, savings in the cost of purchasing larger quantities of direct materials may be affected by taking advantage of quantity discounts. Such discounts would act to reduce variable costs. Either an increase or decrease in variable costs will change the slope of the total cost line on the breakeven chart.

A change in the fixed cost could also occur. At some point in the production process, as the quantity increases, it may be necessary to expand production capacity by, for example, leasing additional space. An increase in the fixed cost of production affects both the fixed cost line and the total cost line on the breakeven chart. Both types of changes are illustrated in Figure 4.8. Note the change in the slope of the total cost curve at point a. At this point, variable cost per unit has decreased. At point c we note an increase in fixed costs causing an abrupt or stepwise increase in both the fixed cost and total cost lines. Also note that these changes result in two breakeven points at points b and d. The change in the slope and position of the total cost curves results in its intersection by the total revenue line at two different points. This simply indicates to management that the cost structure is

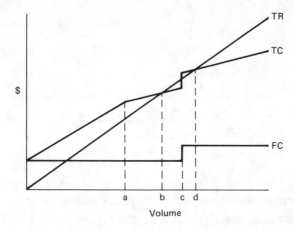

Figure 4.8. Breakeven chart with changes in fixed and variable costs.

such that breakeven can occur at two different production levels. These types of changes are easily accomodated and illustrated by the breakeven chart.

SUMMARY

Breakeven analysis and the breakeven chart provide a simple and convenient technique for analyzing the operations of a business in terms of costs, profits and volume of operation. It is useful in helping management make pricing and investment decisions and for determining and planning for optimal levels of operations. As such it is a valuable tool among those used in the profit maximization program. However, it has its limitations. It is most effective for analyzing a single product or service at a single location. Different products or services should be analyzed using separate breakeven charts each with its prorated share of fixed costs. Attempting to combine several products on a single chart leads to a complicated and confusing device that defeats the purpose of the breakeven chart which is to illustrate the pertinent relationships in a clear and concise manner. And of course, the effectiveness of the chart is dependent upon the accuracy of the information used in constructing it. This means that a good accounting and information processing system is a necessity. Even with these limitations, breakeven analysis is an excellent decision-making and planning tool for the short run.

5. Forecasting

Practically every facet of profit maximization involves the use of accurate information. The importance of a good accounting and information processing system cannot be overemphasized. However, these systems provide historical information while in many instances information about the future is needed. Any planning function requires estimates of future conditions. These functions include, but are not limited to, capacity and materials planning, production planning and scheduling, purchasing, and decisions regarding personnel and inventories. Even the application of breakeven analysis to operating level decisions requires a forecast of demand.

Accurate prophecies have been the desire of mankind through the ages. Oracles, seers and fortune tellers are common in our literature. The ability to make accurate predictions has made heroes out of ordinary men, and the failure to do so has resulted in death for others. Of course, reading tea leaves, gazing into crystal balls, and divinations based on the condition of animal entrails have long gone out of style. Nevertheless, businessmen, politicans, civil servants and managers of all kinds know that the ability to predict future events with reasonable accuracy can still make heroes.

Many mathematicians, statisticians, and economists have devoted their efforts and expertise in attempting to develop scientific methods for predicting the future. Of course, when scientists get involved, it is no longer called predicting; it is called forecasting. The degree to which these methods have been effective varies significantly from application to application. Much of the variability in the results depends upon three factors: the initial assumptions that form the basis for the method, the time horizon or period of the forecast, and the complexity and number of variables involved in the forecast. Considering each of these factors in reverse order, it is much easier to forecast the demand for a single product sold to a relatively small, well-defined, and concentrated market than it is to forecast general economic conditions. The number of variables and their interactions is much greater and more complex in the latter case than in the former. Consequently, the more limited the forecast in terms of the forecast variable, the more accurate it is likely to be.

Furthermore, everything changes with time. The longer the period over which we attempt to forecast, the less accurate the results are likely to be. This is simply due to the fact that the conditions which exist at one point in time and which form the basis for the forecasting model, do not remain constant forever. And the longer the time period involved, the more likely they are to change. Finally, and most obviously, every forecast, regardless of the method used, begins with some set of basic assumptions. If these assumptions are incorrect or inaccurate, the results must inevitably be incorrect or inaccurate also.

In the context of profit maximization, forecasts are used primarily to predict the demand for the product or service provided by the firm. Such demand forecasts enable the manager to establish requirements for productive capacity, personnel, material, and so on without which many of the maximization techniques would be impossible to implement.

Fortunately for the manager of the small or medium-sized business, the forecasts involved in profit maximization need not involve extremely complex conditions nor should they extend over long periods of time. We will discuss some of the most common forecasting methods in this chapter. For convenience we will classify them into three categories: subjective methods, time series methods, and causal methods.

SUBJECTIVE FORECASTING METHODS

Subjective or qualitative methods are not, strictly speaking, scientific methods. For the pure scientist, the ultimate test of his science is its power to predict accurate results stemming from a given set of circumstances irrespective of the individual applying the method. As soon as we allow subjectivity to enter the process, the concept of scientific objectivity must be discarded. However, in forecasting, even with the quantitative methods which will be discussed next, total objectivity is almost impossible to achieve. Therefore, it seems reasonable to include a brief discussion of subjective forecasting methods here.

Subjective forecasting methods typically involve the opinions of so-called experts. One fairly well-known method that relies on the subjective opinions of a panel of experts is called the *Delphi method*. In Delphi, a questionnaire about the future conditions of interest is submitted to the members of the panel. Individual responses to the questionnaire are summarized and then returned to the panel members so that they can revise their original estimates or predictions if they wish to do so. Several rounds of summaries and revisions are possible until some type of consensus is achieved. In this process, the panel members never meet face to face, and therefore no single viewpoint can dominate simply because of the strength of personality or aggressiveness of one member of the panel.

The Delphi method is relatively expensive and is most useful for long-range forecasting of complex economic or technological conditions. It is particularly useful and sometimes the only method available when insufficient historical data exists to use one of the quantitative methods. It is not very well suited to the short-run problems of small and medium-sized businesses and is described here simply because it is one of the best known of the subjective methods.

For the small or medium-sized business, short-run subjective forecasts of demand still rely on expert opinion. In the typical case, the expert or experts are members of the firm doing the forecasting. For example, in a demand forecast the sales manager might make an educated guess, or individual salesmen might submit estimates of demand in their particular areas or territories for some future period. These estimates might then be combined by the sales manager into an overall forecast. Such a procedure can produce a forecast quickly and at a minimal cost to the company. However, the accuracy and efficacy of such forecasts are totally dependent upon the abilities of the individuals participating and are likely to vary considerably from forecast to forecast. It is always helpful to supplement subjective forecasts with data obtained from market studies, customer or consumer surveys, and other sources as time or cost allows. However, for consistency and accuracy some objective, quantitative forecasting method such as one of those described below is recommended.

TIME SERIES METHODS

A time series is a set of numerical observations taken regularly at different points in time. These observations may be in terms of quantities or dollars and generally vary from time period to time period. The basic assumption in time series forecasting is that the variable that we wish to forecast varies regularly as a function of time. This assumption is certainly true for certain types of physical phenomena. For example, the growth of a living organism is certainly a function of time as is radioactive decay. However, the factors of primary interest in profit maximization are economic factors such as sales or demand, production rates, prices, etc. There is no doubt that the values of these variables change with the passage of time, but whether a stable relationship between time and the variable of interest can be determined and used for predicting future values of that variable is still a debatable issue. Nevertheless, for short-term forecasts, time series methods have often proven reasonably accurate and useful provided that the user recognizes their limitations. The theory of the time series is that the movement of a variable over time is influenced by four factors: the trend, the seasonal variation if the data on which the analysis is based are reported for time periods shorter than one year, the cycle if one exists, and random or irregular fluctuations.

The trend refers to the long-term behavior of the variable. The variation of the variable over time due to the trend is the result of gradually changing factors in the environment in which the business operates. Such factors include population growth or decline, social and economic changes in the composition of the population, changes in consumer attitudes and purchasing patterns, technological advances, and so on. Of the four factors in a time series, the trend is the most important in forecasting. If the trend can be identified and isolated from the other factors then it can be extrapolated with caution for short periods and used to predict values of the variable of interest for that period.

Seasonal variation refers to patterns that occur within the period of one year and recur with regularity year after year. The causes of this variability are changes in the weather, the occurrences of holidays, and the conventions or customs of the population. Some examples of variables that exhibit seasonal variation are the demand for heating oil, electric power consumption, and retail sales which tend to peak before certain holidays. Seasonal variation is second in importance to the trend in forecasting for periods of less than a year.

The cycle refers to the business cycle and may or may not exist for a particular variable. When it does exist it is characterized as a periodic growth followed by a decline which repeats itself with regularity over a period of from three to fifteen or more years. When evidence of a cycle is present it is seldom regular enough to be used in forecasting. Furthermore, for short-term forecasting, such as that involved in profit maximization, the cycle would have little or no effect and for practical purposes can be ignored.

Random or irregular variation is due to random causes. Since there is no fixed pattern to its behavior it is unpredictable. When a time series is used for forecasting, the irregular variation is eliminated or smoothed out so that the trend and seasonal components can be studied and described.

In the great majority of cases in small and medium-sized businesses, forecasts for a period greater than one year will concentrate on isolating the trend. These medium-range forecasts would be used for capacity planning, personnel planning, and budgeting. We will use the term *medium range* to refer to forecasts for periods exceeding one year but still within the short run as defined previously. Short-range forecasts for periods of less than a year must also attempt to determine the nature of the seasonal fluctuations. These short-range forecasts are useful in materials planning, purchasing, inventory problems and short-range scheduling.

Classical time series analysis assumes that the four time series components are related to each other multiplicatively. That is the variable to be forecast, call it Y, is equal to the product of the four time series components. Symbolically,

$$Y = T \times S \times C \times I$$

where T equals trend, S is seasonal variation, C is the cycle, and I represents the irregular variation. Given this multiplicative relationship, any single component of the series can be isolated by dividing out the other unwanted factors. for example, if we want to isolate the trend we can divide by the unwanted components as follows:

$$Y = T \times S \times C \times I$$

$$\frac{Y}{S \times C \times I} = \frac{T \times S \times C \times I}{S \times C \times I} = T$$

The classical analysis proceeds by isolating and removing the un-wanted components of the series, one at a time, a process called decomposition. Our simplified procedure will for the time being ignore the unwanted components and attempt to approximate the trend directly and graphically.

For the purpose of illustrating these techniques, we will consider the case of the Atlas Discount Department Store. Sales data compiled annually and by quarters over a ten-year period are shown in Table 5.1. We will use these data in the examples to follow.

Isolating the Trend

Every year, management of the Atlas Discount Department Store prepares a forecast of sales for the coming year. The forecast is used as a basis for decisions that involve the level of business activity, budget preparation, and so on. At the time that next year's forecast is prepared (in this case the 1983 forecast) an estimate is also made for one additional year, 1984. Each year the previous forecast is revised and an additional year is added. Using the annual sales data from the

Table 5.1. The Atlas Discount Department Store; Sales in Hundreds of Thousands of Dollars, 1973–1982.

YEAR	1ST QUARTER	2ND QUARTER	3RD QUARTER	4TH QUARTER	TOTAL
1973	320	334	289	577	1,520
1974	226	507	488	659	1,880
1975	429	637	520	1,014	2,600
1976	583	925	743	1,509	3,760
1977	465	873	774	1,408	3,520
1978	630	1,062	865	1,673	4,230
1979	692	1,249	1,018	1,891	4,850
1980	870	1,306	1,080	2,144	5,400
1981	823	1,387	1,120	2,220	5,550
1982	905	1,350	1,210	2,335	5,800

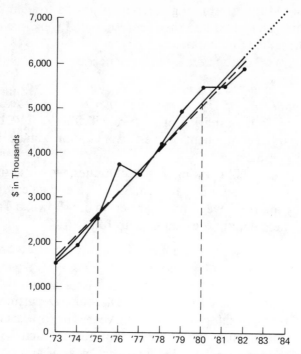

Figure 5.1.   Atlas store sales data 1973–1982 with least squares and semi-average trend lines.

last column of Table 5.1, the points are plotted on the graph shown in Figure 5.1 and the estimated trend line is superimposed.

In Figure 5.1, the horizontal axis is scaled in terms of time. The vertical axis is scaled in terms of dollars or in this case thousands of dollars. The sales corresponding to each year from 1973 through 1982 are plotted with points on the graph. When we connect these points with a series of straight lines it is easy to see that although the points progress in a generally upward direction from the lower left-hand corner to the upper right, the year-to-year behavior is somewhat erratic. Since this plot is of annual data only, there is no seasonal component. Also, although there is some possibility of a cyclical factor, its presence is debatable and unnecessarily complicating. For most businesses, and particularly those in the small and medium-sized categories, it can safely be ignored. Consequently, the series plotted is assumed to consist of the trend and irregular variations. Since the general appearance of the plot seems to suggest a straight line, the simplest procedure for isolating the trend is to fit a straight line to the set of points. The fitted line then represents the trend having eliminated the irregular fluctuations.

It must be mentioned that a trend is not necessarily a straight line. In fact, over the long run the trend is most likely not linear but some other type of curve. Even in the relatively short or medium range, many types of curves have been used to represent trend including the *Gompertz curve* and the *logistic curve*. In analyzing the original plot of points, an initial decision must be made regarding the type of curve that best appears to represent the long-term behavior of the series. The identification of a particular type of curve usually should be left to the judgment of a trained statistician. However, for most short-term forecasts required by the small or medium-sized business, the linear assumption should be adequate.

The problem of isolating the linear trend involves determining the line that best fits the set of points plotted. It is possible to estimate that line subjectively by simply taking a straightedge and drawing a line through the points. The problem with this subjective procedure is that no two individuals will get the same line. An objective criterion devised by statisticians for getting the line of *best* fit is called the *least squares criterion* and results in the *least squares line*. This is a line that minimizes the sum of the squares of the vertical deviations of the individual points from the line. The calculations involved can be tedious and a good objective approximation to the least squares line can be achieved by the method of *semiaverages*. In Figure 5.1 the semiaverage line is the solid straight line while the least squares line, which has also been fitted, is represented by the dashed line. Notice how similar the two lines are to each other. Of course, when a computer is easily available, the least squares line can be computed from packaged programs often supplied by the computer manufacturer or otherwise available. Otherwise the semiaverage line should be quite satisfactory.

The semiaverage line is easy to calculate and can be plotted quickly. The data are divided into two equal parts, a lower half and an upper half, according to time. In the Atlas example, since the data cover ten years the two parts consist of the first five years of annual data, 1973 through 1977, and the second five years, 1978 through 1982. If the data consist of an odd number of years or observations, the middle observation can simply be eliminated.

Two averages are computed, one from each half of the data. We will call these semiaverages $\overline{Y}_1$ and $\overline{Y}_2$. Each average is computed by adding the numerical values of the observations in each half of the data and then dividing by the number of observations added. For Atlas, the semiaverages were computed as follows. Remember that the observations are sales in hundreds of thousands of dollars. The letter Y represents the value of a single observation and the subscript on Y indicates the year. Then:

$$\overline{Y}_1 = \frac{Y_{73} + Y_{74} + Y_{75} + Y_{76} + Y_{77}}{5}$$

$$= \frac{1520 + 1880 + 2600 + 3760 + 3520}{5}$$

$$= \frac{13280}{5} = 2,656$$

$$\overline{Y}_2 = \frac{Y_{78} + Y_{79} + Y_{80} + Y_{81} + Y_{82}}{5}$$

$$= \frac{4230 + 4850 + 5400 + 5550 + 5800}{5}$$

$$= \frac{25830}{5} = 5,166$$

The two semiaverages are plotted on the graph, Figure 5.1, above the middle year or midpoint of the data entering into the average. That is $\overline{Y}_1$ is plotted directly above the year 1975 and $\overline{Y}_2$ above the year 1980. If each half of the data contains an even number of years then the semiaverage is plotted halfway between the two middle years. A straight line is then drawn to connect the semiaverages and is extended to cover all of the years for which the data were plotted.

To forecast sales for 1983 and 1984, the semiaverage trend line is extended or extrapolated. The extrapolated portion of the trend is shown in Figure 5.1 by a dotted line. The estimated sales for those years can be read from the vertical scale. For 1983 the estimate is $6,670,000. For 1984, the estimate is $7,230,000.

Remember that the extrapolation of a trend line can be risky. The further it is extrapolated, the riskier it gets. The rationale behind the extrapolation of a trend is that the factors that acted upon and affected the variable of interest in the past will continue to act and have the same effect in the future. There is of course no assurance that this will be so. Any change in economic or political conditions, technological advances, and so on can have significant effects on the forecast variable changing the slope or direction of the trend line and causing large forecasting errors. The further into the future that a trend is extrapolated, the more likely it is that a change will occur and the greater the potential error in the forecast. This is why Atlas management only forecasts for two years ahead and revises these forecasts annually.

Forecasting Error

There are several different measures of forecast error. These include the *average error,* the *mean squared error,* and the *mean absolute error.* We will use the latter measure here, expressed as a percent.

Forecast error is simply the difference between the value forecast for a period which we will designate F and the true or actual value of the variable for that period designated A. Symbolically the error is

$$E = |A - F|$$

where the two vertical lines represent the absolute value of the difference. That is, the error is the magnitude of the difference without regard to the sign or direction of the difference.

At the time the forecast is made it is impossible to compute the forecast error for 1983 since the actual sales for that year will not be known for at least one year. We can however estimate what the error might be based on the trend line and the actual sales data from the past ten years. This is done in Table 5.2. The values in the column headed Forecast are the trend line values for the years 1973 through 1982. The figures in the Absolute Error Column are the differences, without regard to sign, of the Actual and Forecast values. The Absolute Error column and the Actual Sales column are summed. The *mean absolute error* expressed as a percent is obtained by dividing the sum of the Absolute Errors by the sum of the Actual Sales and then multiplying by 100. Symbolically, this is

$$\text{MAPE} = \frac{\Sigma E}{\Sigma A} \times 100$$

Table 5.2. Forecast Error for Atlas Store Data,
1973–1982

YEAR	ACTUAL	FORECAST	ABSOLUTE ERROR
1973	1,520	1,580	60
1974	1,880	2,065	185
1975	2,600	2,620	20
1976	3,760	3,100	660
1977	3,520	3,645	125
1978	4,230	4,200	30
1979	4,850	4,540	310
1980	5,400	5,025	375
1981	5,550	5,735	185
1982	5,800	6,125	325
	39,110		2,140

where Σ stands for sum and MAPE stands for mean absolute percent error.

For the Atlas forecast,

$$\text{MAPE} = \frac{2140}{39110} \times 100 = 5.47\%$$

The Atlas sales forecast for 1983 by extrapolation was $6,670,000. This forecast is subject to a forecast error of approximately 5.47%. Therefore, Atlas should consider that sales in 1983 should be between $6,670,000 plus and minus $364,849, or between $6,305,151 and $7,034,849, with the most likely value $6,670,000.

A somewhat different application of trend analysis is illustrated in the following example.

The Hunter Manufacturing Company

The Hunter Manufacturing Company is a small manufacturer specializing in the production of precision electronic and electromechanical components under contract to other manufacturers. The production manager of Hunter had previously been concerned about the proportion of defective product issuing from his production lines. He now has encountered an additional problem. The delivery date for a large order of precision parts is fast approaching and he is running behind schedule. One solution might be to order overtime for the production workers involved with that contract. Another might be to shift workers from some other project. However, this second possible solution might only postpone the problem since without the personnel that would have to be moved the other project could also fall behind schedule. The disadvantage of overtime, besides the premium rates that would have to be paid, is that quality, as measured by proportion defective, might deteriorate as the length of the shift increases. An increase in the proportion of defectives produced would also be expensive.

Suppose that a record was kept of the proportion defective produced during each hour of an eight-hour shift. Since this proportion is the variable of interest we will represent it with the letter Y. The letter T represents time. Therefore, each value of T corresponds to the hours 1 through 8 of the shift. The data for one shift are shown in Table 5.3. Figure 5.2 is a graph of these data with the trend line based on semiaverages superimposed. The computation of the semiaverages is shown below.

LOWEST HALF OF THE T VALUES	CORRESPONDING Y VALUE	HIGHEST HALF OF THE T VALUES	CORRESPONDING Y VALUE
1	0.08	5	0.09
2	0.05	6	0.10
3	0.07	7	0.11
4	0.10	8	0.13
	0.30		0.43

$$\overline{Y}_1 = \frac{0.30}{4} = 0.075 \qquad \overline{Y}_2 = \frac{0.43}{4} = 0.108$$

The two semiaverages were plotted on the chart above the values $T = 2.5$ and $T = 6.5$ the midpoints of each set of four values. In order to predict the value of proportion defective for the ninth hour of the shift we must extend the trend line beyond the range of the observed data to a point on the diagram corresponding to $T = 9$. After locating the point on the extrapolated trend line which corresponds to $T = 9$, we can determine the corresponding Y value from the scale on the left. This value is $Y \cong 0.12$ or 12.0%. Based on this trend line, we can

Table 5.3. Hunter Manufacturing Company,
Proportion Defective vs. Time.

HOUR	PROPORTION DEFECTIVE Y
1	0.08
2	0.05
3	0.07
4	0.10
5	0.09
6	0.10
7	0.11
8	0.13

predict that approximately 12% of production will be defective during the first overtime hour, that is the ninth consecutive hour worked.

The reader should realize that in this example we used only eight pairs of observations. We obtained a single value of proportion defective corresponding to each of the eight regular shift hours. This is of

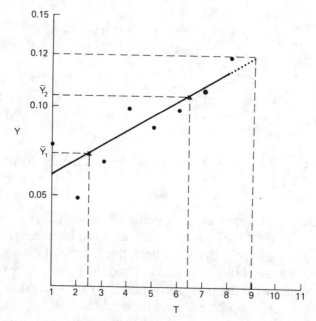

Figure 5.2.   Semiaverage trend line, proportion defective vs. time, Hunter Manufacturing Company.

course an extremely small sample and the results are subject to a considerable sampling error. Also, any manager would have some doubts about drawing a conclusion and making a decision based upon a set of observations obtained from just one shift. Additional data can be obtained and the sample enlarged by *replicating* the experiment. This simply means repeating the experiment or process of observation over several shifts. For example, suppose that the production manager observed and recorded the proportion defective produced hourly on two additional shifts. He would now have three values of proportion defective for hour number 1, three values for hour number 2, and so on, for a total of twenty-four observations. The new data are shown in Table 5.4 and their graph with the semiaverage line superimposed is provided in Figure 5.3. The calculation of the semiaverages from the new data is shown below.

LOWEST HALF OF THE T VALUES	CORRESPONDING Y VALUES	HIGHEST HALF OF THE T VALUES	CORRESPONDING Y VALUES
	0.08		0.09
1	0.04	5	0.07
	0.05		0.08
	0.05		0.10
2	0.06	6	0.08
	0.07		0.12
	0.07		0.11
3	0.05	7	0.10
	0.05		0.11
	0.10		0.13
4	0.08	8	0.11
	0.09		0.12
	0.79		1.22

$$\overline{Y}_1 = \frac{0.79}{12} = 0.066 \qquad \overline{Y}_2 = \frac{1.22}{12} = 0.102$$

Extrapolating the trend line to $T = 9$, the corresponding value of Y is approximately 0.127 or 12.7%. This value is very close to that obtained with the smaller sample; however, the production manager of the Hunter Manufacturing Company should have more confidence in the accuracy of this estimate because of the larger number of observations involved.

Table 5.4. Hunter Manufacturing Company
Proportion Defective vs. Time,
(Three Shifts).

HOUR	PROPORTION DEFECTIVE Y		
T	SHIFT 1	SHIFT 2	SHIFT 3
1	0.08	0.04	0.05
2	0.05	0.06	0.07
3	0.07	0.05	0.05
4	0.10	0.08	0.09
5	0.09	0.07	0.08
6	0.10	0.08	0.12
7	0.11	0.10	0.11
8	0.13	0.11	0.12

Whether the production manager decides to use overtime to meet his production schedule in the light of a possible 12.7% and increasing proportion defective or to borrow personnel from some project should be based on the increased costs and delays that would ensue

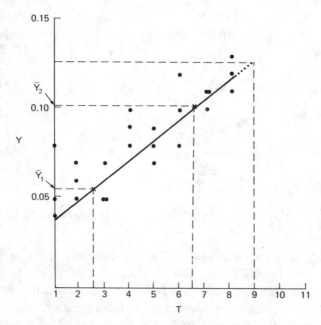

Figure 5.3. Semiaverage trend line, proportion defective vs. time, three shifts, Hunter Manufacturing Company.

from the declining quality of the output on overtime. In making his decision, the production manager should also consider the amount of error inherent in the extrapolation. What that decision should be will not be considered here. The purpose of this example is simply to illustrate the use of a trend analysis for a purpose other than that of predicting demand.

Seasonal Variation

Short-range forecasts are for periods of less than a year. Such forecasts are required for decisions involving inventory levels, purchases, staffing and so on. For forecast periods of less than a year, data must be available for periodic intervals within the year, say by months or quarters. In Table 5.1, sales data for the Atlas Discount Department Store was provided by quarters and we will use those data to illustrate the isolation of the seasonal component of a time series.

Seasonal variation can be expressed and used most easily as a percent of the annual forecast. That is, if Atlas forecasts sales of approximately $6,670,000 for the year 1983, and if seasonal variation is a factor, then management should determine what percent of the annual sales will occur in the first quarter, in the second quarter, and so on. Of course, if there is no seasonal variation whatsoever, then they should expect approximately 25% of total sales to occur in each quarter.

However, Atlas management knows that seasonal factors do affect their sales and therefore the seasonal indexes and percentages should be determined for their short-range forecasts. The simplest method for quantifying the seasonal component of the series is to first isolate it by the method of *moving averages*. A moving average is simply a series of averages computed from the terms in a series by successively dropping one old term and adding one new one for each successive average. For example, in a three-term moving average, the averages are computed from three terms at a time. Each new average drops the first term that went into the previous average and adds the next term in succession in the original series.

For a three-term moving average, after each three successive terms have been averaged, the result is placed to coincide with the middle term used in the average. The procedure is as follows:

$$\frac{Y_1 + Y_2 + Y_3}{3} = \overline{Y_1} \qquad \text{centered at } Y_2$$

$$\frac{Y_2 + Y_3 + Y_4}{3} = \overline{Y_2} \qquad \text{centered at } Y_3$$

$$\frac{Y_3 + Y_4 + Y_5}{3} = \overline{Y_3} \qquad \text{centered at } Y_4$$

and so on.

If an even number of terms is used in the moving average, say a four-term moving average, each average is centered halfway between the two middle terms, that is,

$$\frac{Y_1 + Y_2 + Y_3 + Y_4}{4} = \overline{Y_1} \qquad \text{centered between } Y_2 \text{ and } Y_3$$

$$\frac{Y_2 + Y_3 + Y_4 + Y_5}{4} = \overline{Y_2} \qquad \text{centered between } Y_3 \text{ and } Y_4$$

Moving averages have a tendency to smooth the series by eliminating erratic fluctuations. Consequently, converting the original series to a series of moving averages is often referred to as a *smoothing operation*. The number of terms included in each average determines the degree of smoothing that occurs. Usually, the more terms included in the average, the smoother the results.

Since moving averages smooth a time series by removing the short-term or irregular fluctuations, a moving average applied to monthly or quarterly data will tend to eliminate the seasonal and irregular movements, leaving only the trend and the cycle, if it exists. However, since the presence of a well-defined cycle in most such series is doubtful at best, we will assume that the components of the series are simply trend, seasonal variation and irregular movements. That is,

$$Y = T \times S \times I.$$

Now, if MA represents *moving average,* MA is approximately equivalent to the trend and we can write MA $\cong$ T, where $\cong$ means approximately equal. Then,

$$\frac{Y}{MA} = \frac{T \times S \times I}{T} = S \times I$$

that is, by dividing each value of the series by the moving average we are left with the seasonal and irregular components only.

Of course, having reached this point we are left with $S \times I$ and must still remove I in order to isolate the seasonal component. This is also accomplished with an averaging procedure, but this time we will not use a moving average. The monthly or quarterly values of $S \times I$ are grouped by month or quarter and a *modified mean* is computed for each period. A modified mean is a simple average obtained from a set of data after first eliminating the largest and smallest values in the set.

Once obtained, these modified means multiplied by 100 constitute a set of *unadjusted* seasonal indexes. For a set of monthly data the sum of these twelve seasonal indexes should equal 1200. For quarterly data the sum of the four seasonal indexes should be 400. When the sums obtained by adding the unadjusted indexes do not equal these values, an adjustment must be made. In other words, the sums of the seasonal indexes must be forced to equal 1200 or 400 for the monthly and quarterly data respectively by multiplying each unadjusted index by an adjustment factor. The adjustment factor for the monthly indexes is simply 1200 divided by the sum of the unadjusted indexes. For the quarterly indexes, it is 400 divided by the sum of the unadjusted indexes. The procedure is really quite simple and is summarized as follows:

1. Isolate the trend by computing a series of moving averages.
2. Divide each value in the original series by the corresponding moving average. The result will be a series containing only the seasonal and irregular components.
3. Group this resulting series of $S \times I$ by period.
4. Compute a modified mean for each period.
5. Multiply each modified mean by 100. This is the unadjusted seasonal index for each period.
6. Multiply each unadjusted index by the appropriate adjustment factor. This produces the adjusted seasonal index for each period.

We will use the quarterly data in Table 5.1 to compute quarterly indexes for the Atlas Discount Department Store and then apply them to the 1983 sales forecast. This example will also illustrate the computation of moving averages. In this case we will use three-term moving averages, that is, each moving average will be computed from three successive quarterly values. The data and the results of these computations are shown in Table 5.5. For the sake of simplicity we have used only the last five years of data, that is, the data from 1978 through 1982.

In column 1 of Table 5.5 we have simply listed each year and its four quarters. Column 2 associates the sales figures with the appropriate quarter. Columns 3 and 4 show the two step computation for the three-term moving average. In column 3, each successive set of three values are added with the total placed in line with the middle term. For example, the first figure in column 3 is 2557 which is the sum of 630 + 1062 + 865. The number 2557 is in line with the middle term, 1062. Then the total in column 3 is simply divided by 3 and the result,

Table 5.5. Atlas Discount Department Store; Quarterly Sales in Hundreds of Thousands of Dollars.

YEAR AND QUARTER		SALES	3 QUARTER MOVING TOTAL	3 QUARTER MOVING AVERAGE $MA = T$	$\frac{SALES}{MA} = S \times I$
1978	1st	630			
	2nd	1062	2557	852.3	1.246
	3rd	865	3600	1200.0	0.721
	4th	1673	3230	1076.7	1.554
1979	1st	692	3614	1204.7	0.574
	2nd	1249	2959	986.3	1.266
	3rd	1018	4158	1386.0	0.734
	4th	1891	3779	1259.7	1.501
1980	1st	870	4067	1355.7	0.642
	2nd	1306	3256	1085.3	1.203
	3rd	1080	4530	1510.0	0.715
	4th	2144	4047	1349.0	1.589
1981	1st	823	4354	1451.3	0.567
	2nd	1387	3330	1110.0	1.250
	3rd	1120	4727	1575.7	0.711
	4th	2220	4245	1415.0	1.569
1982	1st	905	4475	1491.7	0.607
	2nd	1350	3465	1155.0	1.169
	3rd	1210	4895	1631.7	0.742
	4th	2335			

the moving average, is entered in column 4. Remember that the moving average is approximately equal to the trend value. By dividing the original value in column 2 by the moving average in column 5 we are left with a value representing the seasonal and irregular components of the series. It is now necessary to remove the irregular component. These computations are shown in Table 5.6.

In Table 5.6 the $S \times I$ values obtained in Table 5.5 are grouped by quarter and the largest and smallest values in each column are crossed out. The modified mean is computed from the remaining values. For example, in the first-quarter column, after the largest and smallest values are crossed out, the remaining two values are added and then divided by 2 giving 0.590. In the second quarter column the three remaining values are added and then divided by 3 giving 1.233. Each of the modified means is then multiplied by 100 resulting in the set of four unadjusted quarterly indexes, 59.0, 123.3, 72.3 and 156.2. The adjustment factor is obtained by adding the four unadjusted indexes and then dividing their sum into 400. That is,

$$59.0 + 123.3 + 72.3 + 156.2 = 410.8$$

and

$$400/410.8 = 0.974$$

Table 5.6. Computation of Quarterly Seasonal Indexes, Atlas Discount Department Store Data.

YEAR	QUARTER (S X I)			
	FIRST	SECOND	THIRD	FOURTH
1978		1.246	0.721	1.554
1979	0.574	1.266	0.734	1.501
1980	0.642	1.203	0.715	1.589
1981	0.567	1.250	0.711	1.569
1982	0.607	1.169	0.742	
Sums	1.181	3.699	2.170	3.123
Modified means	0.590	1.233	0.723	1.562
Unadjusted seasonal index	59.0	123.3	72.3	156.2
Adjusted seasonal index	57.4	120.1	70.4	152.1

which is the adjustment factor. Then each of the unadjusted seasonal indexes are multiplied by 0.974 to obtain the adjusted seasonal indexes which are designated S_1, S_2, S_3, and S_4. That is,

$$S_1 = 59.0 \times 0.974 = 57.4$$
$$S_2 = 123.3 \times 0.974 = 120.1$$
$$S_3 = 72.3 \times 0.974 = 70.4$$
$$S_4 = 156.2 \times 0.974 = 152.1$$

Finally, if each of the adjusted seasonal indexes is divided by the sum of the indexes, in this case by 400, the proportion or percent of annual sales which should, on the average, occur in each period, will result. For example,

57.4/400 = 0.144 or by 14.4%   in the first quarter,
120.1/400 = 0.300 or 30.0%   in the second quarter,
70.4/400 = 0.176 or 17.6%   in the third quarter,
152.1/400 = 0.380 or 38.0%   in the fourth quarter.

From the semiaverage trend line, Atlas' forecast for 1983 was $6,670,000. Applying the seasonal percentages to the annual figure, the quarterly forecasts for 1983 are:

1st quarter: 0.144 × $6,670,000 = $ 960,480
2nd quarter: 0.300 × $6,670,000 = $2,001,000
3rd quarter: 0.176 × $6,670,000 = $1,173,920
4th quarter: 0.380 × $6,670,000 = $2,534,600

It might occur to the reader after going through the previous illustration that this is a somewhat complicated method for obtaining the quarterly percentages. A much simpler approach might simply be to average sales for each quarter over the period covered by the data and determine what proportion the average quarterly sales represents of the average annual sales. However, if this is done, instead of isolating and determining the seasonal effect we have simply averaged data that still contains the effects of the trend and the irregular variations. Consequently, the results are a great deal less accurate than those provided by the method illustrated. To show the discrepancies that result from a simple averaging we have computed quarterly percentages in this way from the same data in order to compare the results with those obtained from the seasonal analysis. The results are as follows:

	QUARTERLY PERCENTAGES BY SEASONAL ANALYSIS	QUARTERLY PERCENTAGES BY AVERAGING
1st Quarter	14.4	15.0
2nd Quarter	30.0	25.0
3rd Quarter	17.6	20.0
4th Quarter	38.0	40.0

	1983 FORECAST BY SEASONAL ANALYSIS	1983 FORECAST BY AVERAGING	DISCREPANCY AS A % OF SEASONAL ANALYSIS FORECAST
1st Quarter	$ 960,480	$1,005,500	+ 4.7%
2nd Quarter	$2,001,000	$1,667,500	− 16.7%
3rd Quarter	$1,173,920	$1,334,000	+ 13.6%
4th Quarter	$2,534,600	$2,668,000	+ 5.3%

Exponential Smoothing

There is, of course, more than one way to do practically anything and that includes forecasting. In the previous section on seasonal analysis, we used moving averages to isolate the trend from the series of quarterly sales figures so that it could be removed leaving the seasonal and irregular variations for further analysis. In discussing trend, the procedure we used for isolating trend was a graphical one. It should be obvious to the reader that trend can be isolated by the method of moving averages as well as by curve fitting and probably in other ways as well.

Moving averages have a smoothing effect on a time series which tends to remove random and seasonal fluctuations and isolate the trend. The larger the number of periods used in the moving average, the greater smoothing effect. However, the more terms included in the moving average, the greater the weight attributed to past performance as compared to more recent data. Conversely, the fewer terms included in the moving average, the more sensitive it will be to recent changes. Selecting the number of terms to be included in the moving average is a matter of judgment and represents the analyst's feeling regarding the relative importance of recent as opposed to more remote events in their effect on the future. Such a judgment was not required when using the graphical method. Furthermore, the moving average method can only be used for forecasting one period ahead.

A forecasting method that has gained considerable acceptance and tends to eliminate some of the disadvantages of the moving average method is called *exponential smoothing*. This is a refinement of the moving average method that allows the effect of old data to be gradually discounted with increasing weight placed on the more recent data. The simplest exponential smoothing method estimates demand for the next period, designated F_{t+1}, by adding or subtracting a fraction, α (alpha), of the difference between the actual current demand, A_t, and the previous forecast for the present period, F_t. That is, the forecast for the next period is equal to alpha times the actual demand in the present period plus 1 minus alpha times the previous forecast for the current period. Symbolically, this can be stated:

$$F_{t+1} = A_t + (1-\alpha)F_t$$

where t represents the current period and $t + 1$ represents the next period to be forecast. The Greek letter α is called the smoothing constant and is a number between 0 and 1, usually in the area of 0.1 to 0.4.

For example, if $\alpha = 0.10$, then the forecast for the next period is equal to 10% of actual sales in the current period plus 90% of the previous forecast for the current period. If $\alpha = 0.40$, then the forecast equals 40% of actual sales in the current period and 60% of the previous forecast for the current period. In the latter case, considerably more weight is attributed to the recent data and less to the older data than when α was 0.10.

Of course, to prepare a forecast using exponential smoothing we need a previous forecast and a value for α. The value of α is based on the analyst's judgment and sometimes on trial and error. When exponential smoothing is used for the first time a previous forecast will not be available. Therefore, for the first forecast period it is necessary to use actual sales or demand instead of forecast sales or demand. That is, for the first forecast, $F_t = A_t$.

For example, suppose that in 1981 Atlas decided to use the exponential smoothing method with α equal to 0.30 to make annual forecasts beginning in 1982. Since this would be the first forecast there would be no F_t. Therefore, the 1982 forecast would be the same as actual sales in 1981. Using the exponential smoothing formula with A_t substituted for F_t we would get

$$F_{1982} = (0.30)A_{1981} + (0.70)A_{1981} = A_{1981} = \$5,550,000.$$

In 1982 actual sales were \$5,800,000.

For the 1983 forecast Atlas can now use both actual sales in 1982 and the forecast for 1982. The forecast for 1983 would then be

$$
\begin{aligned}
F_{1983} &= (0.30)A_{1982} + (0.70)F_{1982} \\
&= (0.30)\,(\$5,800,000) + (0.70)\,(\$5,550,000) \\
&= \$5,625,000.
\end{aligned}
$$

In order to compare different forecasting methods we would have to apply each method to historical data and see how close they come to the actual values recorded. That is, we would compare the forecasting error under both methods. In Table 5.7 we have used the 10 years of annual sales data from Atlas to compare forecasts using the semiaverage trend and exponential smoothing with $\alpha = 0.30$.

For these data, the average percent error using the semiaverage trend was only 5.4%. For the exponential smoothing method with $\alpha = 0.30$ it was over 30%. This comparison is somewhat misleading

Table 5.7. Comparison of Forecasts; Semiaverage Trend and Exponential Smoothing, Atlas Data 1973–1982

YEAR	ACTUAL SALES $'000's	FORECAST BY SEMIAVERAGE TREND LINE	FORECAST ERROR	FORECAST BY EXP. SMOOTHING $\alpha = 0.30$	FORECAST ERROR
1973	1,520	1,580	60		
1974	1,880	2,065	185	1,520	760
1975	2,600	2,620	20	1,628	972
1976	3,760	3,100	660	1,920	1840
1977	3,520	3,645	125	2,472	1048
1978	4,230	4,200	30	2,786	1444
1979	4,850	4,540	310	3,219	1631
1980	5,400	5,025	375	3,708	1692
1981	5,550	5,735	185	4,216	1334
1982	5,800	6,125	325	4,616	1184
	39,110		2,140		11,905

however. For a constantly increasing series, such as Atlas sales were over this ten-year period, the exponentially smoothed forecast will always lag behind the actual values. In the extreme case, letting $\alpha = 1.0$, the forecast for the next period would always be equal to actual sales in the previous or current period. However, for a fluctuating series, the exponential smoothing method will perform much better. There are also more sophisticated and consequently more complicated exponential smoothing models which are not discussed here.

CAUSAL METHODS

It is sometimes possible to relate values of the forecast variable, sales, demand, etc., to some other observable factor that has a direct causal relationship with the factor of interest. For example, retail sales are related to the level of personal disposable income in the population. The demand for housing in a given period is related to the rate of family formation in some previous period, and so on. When a direct causal relationship can be established, knowledge about values of the causing factor, called the *independent variable,* can be used to forecast values of the other factor, called the *dependent variable.* In order to do so however sufficient data must be collected on both variables and the mathematical relationship between them must be determined. The procedure for doing this is called *regression analysis* and the mathematical expression of their relationship is called the *regression equation.*

There are several disadvantages to the use of regression analysis in forecasting for the small or medium-sized business. The first and probably most important is that while such cause-and-effect relationships may exist between broad economic factors in the general economy, they are less likely to be effective in forecasting sales, demand, or other conditions at the level of the individual firm, particularly the small or medium-sized firm.

Second, seldom is the causal relationship limited to a single independent variable. There are usually many factors that affect the level of retail sales or the demand for housing, or whatever variable is to be forecast. The demand for housing in a given period is no doubt related to the rate of family formation in some previous period. However, it is also affected by many other factors such as the interest rate, the unemployment rate, the price of housing and the general level of prices in the economy, and probably several other factors some of which may not even have been identified. When a causal relationship must be established between a dependent variable and more than one independent variable, we have what is called a *multiple regression analysis*. The identification of the independent variables, the determination of the nature of the relationship and the type of regression equation to be used, the measurement of the effect of each of the independent variables, and the computations involved can be very complicated. The first three of these considerations require a trained statistician while the computations generally require a computer. There are of course regression analysis software packages that are available to computer users. But in general the results are often no better, or at least not much better, than those that can be obtained with the simpler methods described previously.

Econometric models are simply complex regression models and, as mentioned previously, are more applicable to the forecasting of general economic conditions rather than the forecasting problems of the individual firm. The same is true of so-called economic indicators. The reader should not take these remarks to mean that these broad economic conditions have no effect on the individual firm. We know that economic conditions have a significant effect on individual businesses. However, for forecasting specific values of sales, demand, or other variables directly applicable to a specific firm, these broad indicators are of less value than data generated internally.

SUMMARY

Accurate forecasts of demand and other factors are essential in the profit maximization program. These forecasts are used in planning for capacity, material, personnel, inventories, etc. The simplest and most effective forecasting methods for the firm are based on data generated within the firm itself. The time series methods illustrated here are simple, useful and effective for short-term forecasting. Causal methods appear to be less effective for the small or medium-sized business because of the complexity of the analysis required and because the causal factors are more likely to apply to broad economic conditions and less likely to relate to the specific forecast variables of the firm. For the small and medium-sized businesses, the simpler methods are generally the most effective.

6. Capacity Planning

The capacity decision is one of the first decisions that the business owner or manager must make in order to begin operations. It is also an integral part of the planning and decision-making process that must be continued throughout the life of the enterprise. The manager must continually address the following questions. How much should we produce? How big must my plant be? When is expansion warranted and to what extent?

Decisions regarding capacity relate to both the short and long term. However, most short-term measures taken to increase or change capacity can be planned for and implemented in a matter of weeks and do not involve the investment of large amounts of capital. Such measures include initiating or discontinuing overtime, adding additional shifts, using subcontractors, taking short-term leases on facilities, and so on.

Short-term capacity-change decisions result from an unexpected change in demand and must be handled by the manager as part of his day-to-day responsibilities. We will not discuss the short-term problem here since for the most part such considerations are covered in other chapters on allocation and scheduling, production control, and human resources. Our major concern here will be capacity planning over the long run. Recall that the long run is a period of sufficient length for all of the process factors to be adjusted including those of plant and equipment.

If the long-range demand forecast predicts continually increasing demand for the product or service and no increase in competition—a somewhat unlikely scenario—then in general the greater the capacity the greater the returns. However, this is not the usual situation. Most firms must contend with fluctuating demand, increasing competition, limits on capital resources, and inaccurate long-range forecasts. Consequently, capacity planning is a critical aspect of profit maximization over the long run.

Capacity planning for the long run relates primarily to the expansion or contraction of the facilities used to produce the firm's output. Of course, at the inception of the enterprise and the beginning of operations it relates to the acquisition of those facilities. And the term *facilities* applies equally well to service and sales organizations as to manufacturing firms.

Long-range forecasts of demand are difficult to make and are inherently inaccurate. Unexpected occurrences such as business recessions, wars, strikes, technical innovations, etc., always affect the forecast. In our previous discussion of forecasting, whether by graphical trend extrapolation or by some other method, it was emphasized that forecasts beyond a period of a year are subject to large errors. When such forecasts are made they should be reevaluated and if necessary revised on a yearly basis. However, if capacity decisions must be made today based on a forecast of conditions, say five years into the future, it is not always easy, or even possible to change them at a later date. A plant under construction cannot easily be discontinued or, once built, disposed of. A five-year lease cannot simply be ignored, and capital equipment acquired may not be easy to sell except at a loss.

Because of the uncertainties inherent in long-range forecasts, when they are used in capacity planning, they should attempt to assess and provide for contingencies. This generally involves the establishment of alternate capacity plans. In most cases, there should be a plan for the most optimistic set of future conditions, one for the most pessimistic set, and a third for a set of conditions that appear to be most likely at the time the plans are made. This means that the overall plan establishes several tracks or courses that the firm may follow. However, having selected one of the tracks, the firm is not necessarily irrevocably committed to that track over the entire planning horizon. It should be possible to review the forecasts periodically and if necessary switch from one track to another within certain limitations imposed by contractual or other practical considerations. For example, if some middle track is selected and in a year it appears that conditions will most closely approximate the more optimistic track, it is frequently possible to revise the plans and make appropriate adjustments. The planning for such contingencies is one of the primary reasons why planning must be a continuing function of management.

In establishing capacity plans, it is necessary to determine the planning horizon, that is, the period covered by the plan. The minimum duration of the capacity-planning horizon should be determined by the lead time required for adding or changing, but primarily adding, capacity. For example, if the lead time required for acquiring a new facility or expanding the present one is two years and management reviews long-range plans annually, the minimum planning horizon should be three years.

BREAKEVEN ANALYSIS

The commitment to add capacity should be implemented only after a thorough economic analysis of the possible alternatives. The analysis should consider the fixed cost of existing capacity, the variable costs of the output, the return or revenue at various levels of output, and the effect of different capacity alternatives on profit. The simplest tool for such an analysis is the breakeven analysis (explained in a previous chapter) in conjunction with the long-range demand forecast.

Consider the case of Westwind, Inc. whose major products are room air conditioners and ventilating fans. The demand for ventilating fans has been relatively stable for several years and the projections are that it will remain at approximately the same level for the next ten years, the period covered by the latest long-range forecast. The demand for room air conditioners however has shown a steady increase since the inception of the business and this increase in demand is expected to continue at approximately the same rate as in the past. Based on the trend line extrapolation shown in Figure 6.1, the most likely demand for Westwind air conditioners is provided by the extention of the trend to the year 1992. An optimistic and a pessimistic forecast are also shown in that figure. These are based on considerations of possible contingencies that might occur during this period as well as an estimate of the probable error in the extrapolated trend. The contingency estimates, which were used to contribute to the optimistic and pessimistic forecasts, although subjective, were based on a thorough analysis of economic and market conditions and the informed judgments of the top executives of the company.

Since Westwind manufactures several models of room air conditioners and may during the period of the planning horizon add or discontinue models, data on costs and prices are essentially average fig-

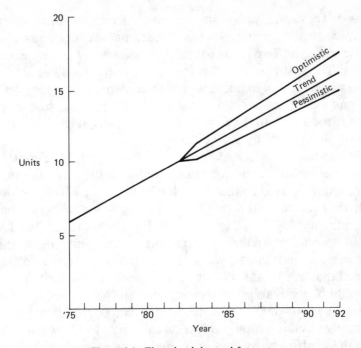

Figure 6.1. Three-level demand forecast

ures for the entire line, adjusted for the estimated effect of inflation. The total capacity of the present plant is 12,000 units per year. West-wind has been producing approximately 10,000 units per year. The forecast for 1983 estimates a demand for 10,800 units. A possible fore-casting error provides a range for that year of between 10,260 and 11,340 units.

The long-range forecast based on Figure 6.1 provides an optimistic, a most likely or trend value, and a pessimistic forecast through 1992, at which time demand is estimated to be between 15,000 and 17,000 units with the trend value at about 15,800. Depending upon which of the three forecast levels are used, the present capacity of 12,000 units will be exceeded in 1984 with the optimistic forecast, in 1986 with the trend, and in 1987 with the pessimistic projection. Given a lead time of approximately two years to acquire additional manufacturing capac-ity, a decision would have to be made immediately if it were based on the optimistic projection. The decision could be delayed for two or three years if based upon either of the other two projections.

At present, the fixed costs allocated to air conditioners are $800,000 per year. The capacity planning decision will be based on an estimated average $350 price per unit sold and an estimated average variable cost of $215 per unit. Two plans for increasing capacity are under consideration. The first plan involves the acquisition of additional capacity in two stages. A new building would be constructed for completion in 1984 and would add an additional 3000 units per year to existing capacity. Production in the new facility would begin in 1984 and fixed costs would increase by $250,000. Then, if the demand forecasts continue to warrant further expansion, an addition would be constructed to add another 3000 units in capacity. Work on the addition would begin sometime in 1985 so that the additional capacity would be available in 1987. Fixed costs after the second expansion would increase by an additional $250,000. This plan will be referred to as Plan 1.

Plan 2 would postpone a decision on capacity until 1984. Then, if the forecast continues to warrant it, a new facility would be constructed that would add 6000 units of capacity at one time. This facility would be ready to go into production in 1986. Fixed costs would increase by $400,000 to a total of $1,200,000. Both plans would eventually result in a total production capacity of 18,000 units which is more than sufficient to meet estimated demand until 1992.

Of course, a third possibility also exists. That is to do nothing and operate with present capacity. This would mean lost sales beginning at that point when demand exceeds Westwind's capability to produce. This is also a viable alternative.

In order to determine which of the three alternatives appears optimal, all should be evaluated under the various estimates of future conditions that appear reasonable, that is, the estimated demand at the three forecast levels, optimistic, the trend, and pessimistic. Although these long-range forecasts have been extended to 1992, the analysis will consider the next five years through 1987 only. This covers all of the capacity changes considered under the three plans and for Westwind represents a more reasonable planning horizon.

There are various methods for analyzing long-range plans such as these capacity plans. For example, we could use the present value of future dollars discounted at some estimated interest rate as a basis for comparing the three plans. Multistage decision trees could also be applied to the analysis for decision making. However, for illustrative purposes, a simple analysis seems to be the most practical and appropriate.

From Figure 6.1 we can find the demand forecast for the years 1983 through 1987. These forecasts of demand in units are shown below.

YEAR	OPTIMISTIC	TREND LINE	PESSIMISTIC
1983	11,340	10,800	10,260
1984	12,005	11,350	10,770
1985	12,670	11,900	11,280
1986	13,335	12,450	11,790
1987	14,000	13,000	12,300

Notice, that since these are linear extrapolations, demand increases by a constant 665 units per year on the optimistic forecast. For the trend and the pessimistic forecasts the increases are a constant 550 and 510 units per year.

Using these figures we will evaluate each of the alternative plans, that is, the Status Quo, Plan 1, and Plan 2. We will begin by assuming the optimistic forecast and looking at each plan under those forecast assumptions.

Optimistic Forecast

Status Quo: With no change in capacity for the next five years, demand will exceed the present capacity of 12,000 units beginning in 1984. The returns to Westwind for each year are computed by taking the number sold times the contribution margin which is $135 per unit ($350–$215) and subtracting the fixed costs. Under the Status Quo, the total returns for the five years are $4,010,900 as follows:

1983	(11,340 × $135) − $800,000 = $	730,900
1984	(12,000 × $135) − $800,000 =	820,000
1985	(12,000 × $135) − $800,000 =	820,000
1986	(12,000 × $135) − $800,000 =	820,000
1987	(12,000 × $135) − $800,000 =	820,000
	Total	$4,010,900

Plan 1: Under this plan Westwind will be able to meet the demand forecast for every year through 1987. Fixed costs will go up in 1984 and again in 1987. The total projected returns for the five years are $3,302,250 as follows:

1983	(11,340 × $135) − $ 800,000 = $	730,900
1984	(12,005 × $135) − $1,050,000 =	570,675
1985	(12,760 × $135) − $1,050,000 =	660,450
1986	(13,335 × $135) − $1,050,000 =	750,225
1987	(14,000 × $135) − $1,300,000 =	596,000
	Total	$3,302,250

Plan 2: With Plan 2, demand will exceed capacity in 1984 and 1985. Then capacity will jump an additional 6000 units in 1986 with a corresponding increase in fixed costs. Total projected returns for five years are $3,661,125 as follows:

1983	(11,340 × $135) − $ 800,000 = $	730,900
1984	(12,000 × $135) − $ 800,000 ≐	820,000
1985	(12,000 × $135) − $ 800,000 =	820,000
1986	(13,335 × $135) − $1,200,000 =	600,225
1987	(14,000 × $135) − $1,200,000 =	690,000
	Total	$3,661,125

In comparing the three capacity plans, returns are highest over this five-year period if the Status Quo is maintained even though some potential sales are lost in the years 1984 through 1987. Since the Status Quo is best under the optimistic forecast it will also be best under the other two forecasts since those estimates of demand are lower. Therefore, further analysis is unnecessary in this case.

What this analysis indicates is not that productive capacity should not be increased in the future but simply that no action to increase capacity should be taken at this time, i.e., 1982. Each succeeding year, as the forecast is revised, the capacity analysis should be repeated. At some point, if demand continues to increase, the decision to add additional capacity might be optimal.

CAPACITY PLANNING IN SALES AND SERVICE ORGANIZATIONS

Capacity planning and analysis for sales and service organizations is practically identical to that for manufacturing companies. At some point in time existing facilities may be inadequate to satisfy demand

and a decision must be made as to when and how much productive capacity should be added. The only major differences between these types of businesses and manufacturing is that the lead time required to acquire additional capacity is generally less than for a manufacturing organization. This generality is based on the assumption that a new facility could more easily be leased and that a new construction would not be necessary. However, lead time will vary and in some instances, a department store, for example, the previous statement may not apply.

Capacity planning decisions rely heavily on demand forecasts and on the type of cost, profit, and breakeven analysis previously described. Without these tools to describe the operating characteristics of the firm and to predict future demand, the planning function would be pure guesswork.

DECISIONS AND RISKS

In the Westwind capacity planning example, we found that even under the most optimistic forecast, the best plan was to maintain the status quo for the present. That is, plan to add no new capacity unless new or revised forecasts change significantly from the present one. Consequently, if no new capacity is required under the optimistic forecast it is obvious that no new capacity would be required under the less optimistic demand estimates either. Therefore, the decision made by Westwind at this time would be the same for all three levels of demand forecast. This will not necessarily always be the case.

There could be situations in which the optimal plan will differ depending upon the demand forecast. In other words, the same plan will not necessarily be optimal for all levels of demand. For example, the analysis might indicate that Plan 1 provides the greatest potential return under the optimistic forecast while Plan 2 is best under the medium or trend forecast and the Status Quo is preferable under the pessimistic forecast. How is a decision made in such a case?

To illustrate we will use another set of figures. Suppose that under an analysis similar to that conducted for Westwind, the potential returns to the company under three different capacity plans for each of three forecast levels are as follows:

Capacity Plan

FORECAST LEVEL	STATUS QUO	PLAN 1	PLAN 2
Optimistic	$4,000,000	$4,400,000	$4,900,000
Trend	$3,425,000	$3,750,000	$3,600,000
Pessimistic	$3,020,000	$3,000,000	$2,750,000

Under this situation, the decision to adopt one of the capacity plans would depend upon which of the forecast levels we consider. Notice that under the optimistic forecast, Plan 2 with estimated returns of $4,900,000 appears to be superior to the other alternatives. On the other hand, with the trend forecast, Plan 1 provides the highest returns. Finally, with the pessimistic forecast, the Status Quo is best. How should a capacity plan be determined?

The manager must remember that in making any decision where the consequences depend on uncertain future events, there is always some risk of making a wrong, or suboptimal, decision. Risks are inherent in any decision-making process under conditions of uncertainty and cannot be eliminated. The prudent manager should of course attempt to minimize these risks. In fact, minimizing decision-making risks is part of the process of maximizing profits. There are several criteria for making decisions under conditions of uncertainty. We will describe several of the simplest and most common.

Maximax

Maximax is short for maximize the maximums. Under this criterion, the manager should determine the maximum return for each of the alternative plans and then select that plan which corresponds to the maximum of the set of maximums. If we were to draw a circle around the maximum return under each of the three capacity plans the set of maximums would be:

	STATUS QUO	PLAN 1	PLAN 2
Optimistic	$4,000,000	$4,400,000	$4,900,000
Trend	$3,425,000	$3,750,000	$3,600,000
Pessimistic	$3,020,000	$3,000,000	$2,750,000

The maximax criterion says that we should select the action corresponding to the maximum of the set of maximums. Since the largest of the three circled values is $4,900,000 and corresponds to Plan 2, under this criterion, Plan 2 should be selected.

Of course, Plan 2 will be optimal only if the optimistic forecast turns out to be the correct one, and that won't be known for several years. In choosing the maximax criterion on which to base his decision, the manager should feel very strongly that future demand will be best approximated by the optimistic forecast. In other words, he should be very optimistic about future demand for his product. The maximax criterion is often referred to as the criterion of optimism.

Maximin

If there is a decision criterion for optimists, it only seems right that there should also be a decision criterion for pessimists. And of course there is. It is called *maximin*. Under this criterion, the manager should determine the minimum return for each of his options and then select the one that corresponds to the maximum of the set of minimums. Drawing circles around the minimum return under each of the three capacity plans, the set of minimums would be:

	STATUS QUO	PLAN 1	PLAN 2
Optimistic	$4,000,000	$4,400,000	$4,900,000
Trend	$3,425,000	$3,750,000	$3,600,000
Pessimistic	$3,020,000	$3,000,000	$2,750,000

Since the maximum of the set of minimums is $3,020,000 and corresponds to the Status Quo, this is the plan that should be selected under maximin. Once again, it should be obvious that this plan will be optimal only if the pessimistic forecast is correct. In selecting this criterion for making his decision, the manager should feel strongly that the pessimistic forecast is the most likely of the three to occur.

The Most Likely Estimate

At this point the reader might, and in fact should, criticize both of the previous criteria as being too simple and too obvious. After all, it doesn't take a great deal of analysis to conclude that if the manager believes that the optimistic forecast is correct he should select the plan that maximizes returns under that assumption. Or, if he believes that the pessimistic forecast is the correct one he should select the plan that will be best under that assumption. This is certainly true, and most managers do indeed make decisions in that way. The weakness in this procedure comes in selecting an optimistic or a pessimistic or some other forecast on which to base the decision. This selection is at best intuitive and at worst simply guesswork. A better method for analyzing and selecting among the alternatives would certainly be desirable. Such a method will be described shortly. At this point, for the sake of completeness we will illustrate the manager's choice if he strongly believes that the trend is the most likely of the three demand levels to occur.

To be consistent with the two previous decision criteria, the manager should maximize returns by selecting the alternative that coincides with the maximum return under whatever demand forecast he believes is most likely. If this happens to be the trend line estimate, then the maximum return is $3,750,000 which coincides with Plan 1.

The Criterion of Neutrality

It isn't easy for any manager to make a choice between three demand level forecasts. Whichever one he chooses for whatever reason, he is likely to be wrong. In fact, because of forecasting error, no specific forecast value is likely to be exactly correct. Therefore, rather than basing a decision entirely on one forecast level and excluding the possibility that one of the others will occur, a better decision criteria would take all of the forecast values into consideration. One such criterion would be the criterion of neutrality. It is given that name because it reflects an attitude of neutrality on the part of the manager with respect to the occurrence of any of the forecasts. In a sense, he considers that all of the forecast levels are equally likely to occur. Consequently, he uses a simple unweighted average to select the best of the capacity plans under all of the forecasts. In this case, since there are three forecast levels, the estimated returns of each plan for the three forecast levels are added and divided by three as follows:

	STATUS QUO	PLAN 1	PLAN 2
Optimistic	$4,000,000	$4,400,000	$4,900,000
Trend	$3,425,000	$3,750,000	$3,600,000
Pessimistic	$3,020,000	$3,000,000	$2,750,000
Sum	$10,445,000	$11,150,000	$11,250,000
Average	$ 3,481,667	$ 3,716,667	$ 3,750,000

Under this criterion, the manager should select the plan that corresponds to the highest of the unweighted averages. In this case, that would be Plan 2.

The Expected Value Criterion

All of the decision criteria discussed so far have one desirable characteristic in common: they are very simple to apply. Under certain conditions, they can also be useful in assisting the manager in choosing a particular alternative from some set of possible alternatives. However, all these criteria are very limited in allowing the manager to express his subjective assessments regarding the likelihood of occurrence of the different demand forecasts. These criteria are essentially all or nothing. Either the manager must select one of the forecasts as being sure to happen to the exclusion of the others and then act on that assumption, or he must be entirely neutral. In terms of likelihoods or probabilities, the manager either assigns a probability of one to one of the forecasts and a probability of zero to all of the others, or he assigns equal probabilities to all of the forecasts. However, these procedures may not reflect his true feelings.

A much more useful criterion would allow the manager to assign other probability values to each of the demand level forecasts which are more consistent with his assessment of their relative likelihoods of occurring. If a probability value of 1 represents certainty and a probability value of 0 represents impossibility, then a value between 0 and 1 would represent the relative likelihood of a particular occurrence. For example, a probability of 0.5 assigned to some event means that the event is just as likely to occur as it is not to occur. A probability of 0.75 means that the event is three times as likely to occur as not to occur. Therefore, if the manager can assess these likelihoods in terms of probabilities, he can use the expected value criterion to select the best of the capability plans.

The expected value of an action is simply a weighted average of the consequences of that action. In this case the consequences are the returns under each of the plans and the weights are the probabilities assigned to the forecast levels. When the expected value of each alternative is computed, the one with the highest expected value is selected.

Consider the three capacity plans and the three forecast levels. Suppose the manager assigns the following probabilities to the forecast levels:

$$
\begin{array}{ll}
\text{Optimistic} - & 0.15 \\
\text{Trend} \quad\;\; - & 0.60 \\
\text{Pessimistic} - & \underline{0.25} \\
& 1.00
\end{array}
$$

Note that the sum of the probabilities assigned to all of the possible conditions is equal to one. The data and the expected values are:

FORECAST	PROBABILITY	STATUS QUO	PLAN 1	PLAN 2
Optimistic	0.15	$4,000,000	$4,400,000	$4,900,000
Trend	0.60	$3,425,000	$3,750,000	$3,600,000
Pessimistic	0.25	$3,020,000	$3,000,000	$2,750,000
	1.00			
Expected Value		3,410,000	$3,660,000	$3,582,000

Since Plan 1 with an expected value of $3,660,000 is the highest of the three, under this criterion, Plan 1 should be adopted.

The expected values were computed as follows:

For Status Quo: $(0.15 \times 4,000,000) + (0.60 \times 3,425,000) + (0.25 \times 3,020,000) = 3,410,000$

For Plan 1: $(0.15 \times 4,400,000) + (0.60 \times 3,750,000) + (0.25 \times 3,000,000) = 3,660,000$

For Plan 2: $(0.15 \times 4,900,000) + (0.60 \times 3,600,000) + (0.25 \times 2,750,000) = 3,582,000$

Since the highest of the three expected values corresponds to Plan 1, that plan should be adopted under this criterion.

Of course, the results obtained are dependent on the probability values assigned by the manager. Consequently, the expected value criterion puts a great deal of emphasis on the manager's judgment in assessing the likelihoods of future conditions. Suppose that instead of assigning probabilities of 0.15, 0.60, and 0.25 to the three forecasts, the manager assigned probabilities of 0.35, 0.50, and 0.15. The results would be considerably different.

FORECAST	PROBABILITY	STATUS QUO	PLAN 1	PLAN 2
Optimistic	0.35	$4,000,000	$4,400,000	$4,900,000
Trend	0.50	$3,425,000	$3,750,000	$3,600,000
Pessimistic	0.15	$3,020,000	$3,000,000	$2,750,000
	1.00			
Expected Value		3,565,000	$3,865,000	$3,927,000

With this new set of probability assessments, Plan 2 has the highest expected value and is the one that should be adopted.

ASSESSING PROBABILITIES

Probability is a measure of uncertainty. Consequently, in any situation where results are contingent on uncertain events, a probability value is the best measure of the relative uncertainty that can be associated with those events. In some cases probability values can be obtained from totally objective considerations: the probability of getting a head on a single toss of a coin, for example, or the probability that when two dice are tossed the sum of the spots on the uppermost faces will equal seven, for another. However, in most business situations the events of interest are usually unique and nonrecurring phenomena, and only subjective assessments of their probabilities are possible. The validity of such assessments is dependent upon the knowledge and ability of the individual making them and on the amount of pertinent subjective information he can draw upon.

Subjective information is information or knowledge possessed by an individual that cannot be verified or substantiated with objective or empirical evidence. The weakness of subjective information in decision making lies in its interpretation not in its lack of substantiation. Everyone receives information from many different sources constantly. Some of these sources are empirical, but many are not. The latter include observations, overheard conversations, impressions and so on. All these inputs are evaluated and stored in memory. This is information in the same sense as any empirical data that we can obtain, and it is useful or useless, good or bad, valid or invalid, depending upon our interpretation of it.

For example, a layman could observe a team of physicians performing a surgical procedure in a hospital operating room. The observer would receive many impressions about what was happening. However, not having any medical training and knowing nothing about operating room procedures, his interpretation of these impressions would be next to worthless. On the other hand, a production manager with many years of experience could walk into a manufacturing plant and observe operations and make judgments that would be extremely accurate. In the latter case, the production manager's store of information received represents a very valuable source of decision-making data about that particular operation. A manager can use the subjective information in his own area of experience and expertise in assigning probabilities to uncertain events in such decision situations.

Converting this subjective information into numerical values of probability is not always an easy task, particularly for a manager who has not been exposed to formal training in probability theory. However, there are devices that can be used to make the transformation from subjective information to numerical probability values easier. The most useful of these devices is the concept of betting odds.

Practically everyone is familiar with the concept of odds. Even people who have never gambled know at least in a vague sort of way what odds represent. If you give 2 to 1 odds on a bet you must risk 2 units of value in order to win one. Therefore, odds are closely related to the stakes, or the amount at risk, in a betting situation.

Odds are also related to the probability of winning. An event for which the odds are 10 to 1 in favor is a great deal more likely to occur than an event for which the odds are only 2 to 1. And the latter event is in turn more likely to happen than another event for which the odds are only 1 to 2 in favor. Of course odds can be quoted in favor of an event or against the event. We will always specify odds in favor of or "for" the event of interest.

When odds are quoted for or against some event, it is usually in the context of betting. This is no doubt because it is gamblers who have adopted this measure of probability for placing bets and making payoffs. The more able a gambler is in assessing odds, the more successful he is likely to be and the more money he will win.

Since most businessmen or business managers do not consider themselves to be gamblers, we seldom hear odds stated in business or investment situations. However, managers must make decisions under conditions of uncertainty similar to those under which gamblers place bets. Therefore, when uncertain events must be evaluated in terms of probability, as is the case here where a capacity plan must be selected under uncertain future conditions, odds provide a convenient method for making the necessary probability assessments.

Odds are convenient and useful because they can be interpreted and expressed in terms of the dollar amount of payoff that an individual would receive in return for a specified number of dollars bet on an event, if that event actually occurs. If the event fails to occur, the bettor's payoff would be negative, that is, he would incur a loss. For example, if you make a bet at odds of 4 to 1 and win, your payoff would be $4.00 for every $1.00 you bet. However, if you bet at odds of 1 to 4 and win, you would receive only $1.00 for every $4.00 you bet. In other words, in order to get someone to take a bet on an event with odds of 1 to 4, you would have to risk $4.00 for the opportunity to win $1.00, while the other bettor would be risking only $1.00 for the opportunity to win $4.00.

Now let's consider how odds can be converted to probabilities. A probability, as we have already mentioned, is a number between 0 and 1 inclusive and can be expressed as a fraction. This can be either a proper fraction such as 7/10 or a decimal fraction such as 0.7. Any decimal fraction can easily be converted to a proper fraction and vice versa. If we start with a probability expressed as a decimal fraction such as 0.7, the first step in converting the value to odds for an event is to state it as a proper fraction, 7/10. A probability presented in this form can be expressed in words as follows: "The chances of the event occurring are 7 out of 10." Now if an event has 7 chances in 10 of occurring it must have 3 chances in 10 of not occurring. Therefore, the odds in favor of the event are 7 to 3. And of course the odds against the event are 3 to 7.

The odds for an event are expressed as the ratio of two numbers which represent the number of chances in favor of the event to the number of chances against its occurrence.

For most people it is much easier to express their subjective assessment of probability in terms of odds first and then convert to probability than it is to assess the probability directly. Once a manager has established his subjective odds for an event the probability expressed as a proper fraction is easily determined. This is done by constructing a fraction with the two numbers in the odds ratio added together and placed in the denominator of the fraction. The single number that refers to the chances in favor of the event is placed in the numerator. That is:

$$\text{Probability for event} = \frac{\text{chances in favor}}{\text{chances in favor} + \text{chances against}}$$

For odds of say 7 to 3, the corresponding probability is

$$\frac{7}{7+3} = \frac{7}{10} = 0.7.$$

Now how should a manager determine whether he believes that the odds in favor of some event are 7 to 3 or 4 to 1 or 65 to 35? The best method for assessing subjective odds, particularly in a nonrecurring, one-of-a-kind situation, is to relate them to the monetary risk he would be willing to assume in betting on that event.

Suppose that during the next football season the Philadelphia Eagles will play one game against the Washington Redskins. If the odds favor the Eagles by 2 to 1, what does that mean to a potential bettor? First, it means that if the odds are correct, it would be reasonable to risk $2.00 betting on the Eagles in order to have the opportunity of winning $1.00 from someone betting on the Redskins. Or conversely, it would be reasonable to risk $1.00 betting on the Redskins for a chance to win $2.00 from someone betting on the Eagles. In either case, these odds express the relative likelihood of either team winning the game. On the basis of these odds, the Eagles are twice as likely to win as the Redskins and the Redskins are half as likely to win as the Eagles.

If the Eagles are twice as likely to win as the Redskins, their chances of winning the game are 2 out of 3 and their probability of winning is

$$\frac{2}{2+1} = \frac{2}{3} = 0.67.$$

Whether in gambling or in business situations that require decisions under conditions of uncertainty, the subjective probability of an event can be determined from the amount that the decision maker would be willing to risk by acting on the assumption that an uncertain event will occur in conjunction with the potential gains or losses that might result. In using probabilities to weigh payoffs or returns and to compute expected values, it is most convenient to use probabilities expressed as decimal fractions. Therefore, whenever the manager makes his initial assessment in terms of odds, the odds should be converted to the probabilities as decimal fractions.

For a manager faced with a capacity-planning decision, or for that matter, any decision whose outcome is dependent upon the occurrence of some uncertain future event, assessing probabilities by determining odds is a useful procedure. It is easier to determine the amount of money you would be willing to risk on an uncertain event in exchange for an opportunity to gain some other sum of money than it is to assess the probability of the uncertain event directly. Consider as another example a bet that you might be tempted to make on a championship boxing match. You are considering making a bet on fighter B to win the fight over fighter A. If you would be willing to bet $1.00 in order to win $1.00 your assessment of the odds for fighter B to win are 1 to 1. The probability that you assign to the event that fighter B wins the fight is:

$$\frac{1}{1+1} = \frac{1}{2} = 0.50$$

On the other hand, if you would refuse to bet on fighter B at even money but would be willing to risk $1.00 only if you have the opportunity of winning $2.00, then you have assessed the odds for B at 1 to 2. The corresponding probability that B will win is:

$$\frac{1}{1+2} = \frac{1}{3} = 0.33$$

If you were quite certain that B would win and would be willing to bet $2.00 in order to win $1.00 then your odds for B would be 2 to 1 and the corresponding probability is:

$$\frac{2}{2 + 1} = \frac{1}{3} = 0.67$$

The process that an individual follows in arriving at a set of betting odds that represent his probability estimates is difficult to explain. Each individual probably bases his assessments on his store of subjective information. In the prize fighting example, this information probably includes what the potential bettor knows or thinks he knows about the two fighters. That information probably results from what he has read or heard or observed about their experience, their records and their physical abilities. The final assessment of odds and probabilities results from a conscious or a subconscious evaluation of this information. The more information that has been accumulated about the subject, the better the assessment is likely to be.

In some decision situations, the manager is concerned with the occurrence or nonoccurrence of a single event, or, what amounts to the same thing, the occurrence of one of only two possible, mutually exclusive events. In the latter statement, the second event simply corresponds to the nonoccurrence of the first. When this is the case, the manager need only determine the odds for one of the events. Once the odds for one event are specified, the odds for the other are automatically fixed. That is, if there are only two events, A and B, and B must occur if A fails to occur, then the odds for A are the same as the odds against B and vice versa. For example, if the odds are 4 to 1 for A then the odds must be 1 to 4 for B. The respective probabilities of A and B are therefore 0.80 and 0.20.

When there are more than two mutually exclusive events for which probabilities must be assessed, the procedure is not quite as simple. The odds for each event should be assessed separately, converted to probabilities, and then adjusted so that the sum of the probabilities of all the events equals 1.

This procedure can best be illustrated by returning to the three levels of demand in the example regarding alternate capability plans. These levels were referred to as optimistic, trend, and pessimistic. The estimated returns for each of three capability plans were dependent upon which of the three demand levels was assumed. In determining the optimal plan we recommended the expected value criterion which requires that probabilities be assigned to each forecast level. In order to assess these probabilities, the manager should address each of the three demand levels separately and assess his subjective odds for that particular level occurring. Since there are three possible levels, the manager should first consider whether he believes that they are all equally likely to occur. If he truly believes that they are all indeed equally likely he should then assign a probability of 1/3 or 0.33 to each of the levels.

Suppose however that the manager believes that the trend forecast is the most likely. In fact, he feels that he would be more than willing to bet a dollar on the event at even money. On further consideration, he decides that he would be willing to risk a dollar on that assumption if his potential payoff was less than one dollar. Analyzing his feelings further he concludes that he might be willing to bet $2.00 on that event in order to win only $1.00. If that is the case, then his odds for that event are 2 to 1. Still analyzing his feelings he finally decides that he is not quite that certain and therefore would risk $3.00 in order to win $2.00. Consequently, his final assessment of his odds in favor of the trend forecast occurring are 3 to 2. The corresponding probability is therefore 3/5. We will leave this probability in fractional form for the time being.

Turning to the pessimistic forecast, he feels much less confident about its occurrence. In fact, he would only be willing to bet $1.00 on that event if he could win $3.00. His odds for the pessimistic forecast are 1 to 3 and the corresponding probability is 1/4.

Finally, considering the optimistic forecast, the manager believes that this is even less likely than the pessimistic one. He decides that he would be willing to risk $1.00 only if he could win $4.00. His odds are 1 to 4 and the corresponding probability is 1/5.

Summarizing his assessments for the three forecast levels we have:

OPTIMISTIC	TREND	PESSIMISTIC
$\dfrac{1}{5}$	$\dfrac{3}{5}$	$\dfrac{1}{4}$

Since the sum of all of the probabilities of all the possible events must equal 1, we will have to add these probabilities and see if they indeed do sum to 1. To do so, we must first determine the lowest common denominator for the three fractions that we want to add. This is the lowest number that can be evenly divided by the denominators of all of the fractions entering into the sum. In this case the lowest common denominator is 20, the smallest number that can be evenly divided by 4 and 5. The equivalent fractions having the common denominator are easily obtained by dividing the present denominator of each fraction into the lowest common denominator and then multiplying the numerator of that fraction by the result of the division. The answer is then placed over the lowest common denominator. Following this procedure we get:

OPTIMISTIC	TREND	PESSIMISTIC
$\dfrac{4}{20}$	$\dfrac{12}{20}$	$\dfrac{5}{20}$

These new fractions are equivalent to the original fractions.

The sum of the three probabilities expressed as proper fractions is

$$\frac{4}{20} + \frac{12}{20} + \frac{5}{20} = \frac{21}{20}$$

Since this sum is greater than one, an adjustment must be made to force the sum to equal 1. This is done by multiplying each fraction by the reciprocal of the sum. The reciprocal of a fraction is obtained by reversing the numerator and the denominator. The reciprocal of 21/20 is 20/21. Carrying out this adjustment and then converting each adjusted proper fraction to a decimal fraction we get:

$$\text{Optimistic:} \quad \frac{4}{20} \times \frac{20}{21} = \frac{80}{420} = 0.19$$

$$\text{Trend:} \quad \frac{12}{20} \times \frac{20}{21} = \frac{240}{420} = 0.57$$

$$\text{Pessimistic:} \quad \frac{5}{20} \times \frac{20}{21} = \frac{100}{420} = 0.24$$

$$\text{Sum} \quad \overline{1.00}$$

The three probabilities now add up to 1. The manager can now use these probabilities in computing expected values or he could round them to a more even set of numbers. Notice that in the previous examples, the probabilities used for the optimistic, trend, and pessimistic forecasts were respectively 0.15, 0.60, and 0.25. If the probabilities of 0.19, 0.57, and 0.24 were used to compute expected values for the three capacity plans, the results would be:

Status Quo:	$3,437,050
Plan 1:	$3,701,100
Plan 2:	$3,643,000

Since the expected returns with Plan 1 are the highest of the three the decision would be to select Plan 1; the same decision reached with the slightly different set of probabilities.

Suppose that the probabilities determined above were rounded to the values 0.20, 0.55, and 0.25 and the expected values of the three plans computed again. The results would be:

Status Quo:	$3,438,750
Plan 1:	$3,700,500
Plan 2:	$3,647,500

And the decision would be the same. We can see that the three slightly different sets of probabilities result in exactly the same decision, that is, adopt Plan 1. This would indicate that the expected value decision criterion is not terribly sensitive to small changes in probabilities. Therefore, although the manager should conscientiously attempt to reflect his subjective feeling in these assessments as accurately as possible, absolute precision is not necessary even if it were possible.

IMPLICATIONS TO PROFIT MAXIMIZATION

Capacity-planning decisions have important implications with respect to the goal of profit maximization. However, these decisions do not have an effect independent of other decisions made with respect to other functions and operations of the firm. They do, in fact, interface with various other operations. For example, they interface with marketing in terms of product mix and promotion. They affect and are affected by technological decisions in terms of both products and processes. Since capacity decisions commit resources over a long period of time, they also affect and are affected by financial planning decisions and financial resources. Finally, they affect the goals and philosophy of the firm with regard to its size, place in the market, quality of product and so on.

Although long range forecasts are difficult to make and inherently unreliable, they are the only basis for making capacity plans and decisions. Frequent revision of such forecasts and analysis of the risks involved should be a part of the forecasting process, but in the final analysis, decisions about the future must be made and should be based on the best information available at the time. With the forecasts as a given requirement, capacity planning serves to clarify the options available to managers. There is seldom a single right answer or right decision. However, with the tools available, the manager can make rational decisions that should contribute to the goal of long-range profit maximization.

SUMMARY

Capacity planning is that part of the planning function that will determine how much the firm will be able to produce over the long run. Without such plans the firm will be faced with too much or too little capacity or alternating periods of one and then the other. Both conditions contribute to profit erosion either through lost business or through idle capacity.

Capacity plans are highly dependent on long-range demand forecasts and on a clear picture of the operating characteristics of the firm under varying levels of output. Because of the unreliability of most long-range forecasts, several levels of demand should be considered in selecting the capacity plan. This requires that capacity-planning decisions take into consideration uncertain future events, a situation that makes decision making difficult. A useful aid for decision making under such circumstances is the expected value criterion based on subjective assessments of the probabilities of the uncertain events.

7. Optimizing Inventories

Mismanaged inventories represent one of the major causes of profit erosion in all types of businesses except for service organizations. In businesses that provide services to the public, inventories consist primarily of supplies; thus, problems of shortages, obsolescence and so on have little effect on profits. In all other types of businesses (manufacturers, retailers, wholesalers, etc.), inventories represent substantial investments, and inventory decisions and policies can have a significant effect on profits.

The basic inventory problems involve questions of how much to stock and when and how much to order. The wrong answers to these questions can result in shortages, delays, and lost business on the one hand and obsolete or unnecessarily large stocks of material on the other.

The two major types of costs associated with inventories are carrying costs (the costs associated with holding material in inventory) and ordering costs (the costs of acquiring material for inventory). Carrying costs can be lowered by ordering frequently and retaining small quantities in inventory. Ordering costs can be reduced by ordering infrequently and maintaining large inventories. Obviously, as one type of cost is decreased, the other increases. The goal of an optimal inventory policy is to keep total costs to a minimum. For the time being, we will assume that total inventory costs are the sums of carrying costs and ordering costs. Another type of cost, shortage costs, will be considered later.

It should be obvious that every type of business has many different inventories, that is, inventories of different items and materials. The Butler Shoe Company, for example, has separate inventories of men's, ladies', and children's shoes. Within each of these categories there are inventories of different sizes, different styles and different brands. Westwind, Inc. maintains inventories of the various parts, components and raw materials necessary to manufacture its air conditioners and ventilating fans. It also has inventories of finished product waiting to be shipped to customers. For each different item in inventory, or stated differently, for each inventory of a particular item, the same problem exists: when and how much to order to keep total costs at a minimum. Consequently, when discussing inventory policies with respect to a particular item or type of material, the reader should realize that the discussion refers to only one of the many inventories maintained by the firm. However, the same procedures for optimization can and should be applied to each of the individual inventories. If optimal inventory procedures are applied to each inventory separately, then the overall inventory situation will tend to become optimized.

FACTORS IN INVENTORY MANAGEMENT

An inventory is a stock of goods held by the firm for future production or sale. In many companies, inventory is one of the most expensive assets and can often represent as much as forty percent of total invested capital. If inventory is not effectively controlled, the costs to the firm can be extremely high and can have a significant adverse effect on profits.

As mentioned previously, three types of costs are associated with inventories: ordering costs, carrying costs, and shortage costs. Ordering costs are those costs incurred in ordering and receiving merchandise for inventory. Included in this category are salaries paid to purchasing and some accounting personnel and wages paid to workers in the receiving and warehousing areas. It also includes transportation charges on the shipments of material for inventory. If the firm is a manufacturing organization and produces all or some of its inventory, production or setup costs are considered to be the same as ordering costs. For proper inventory control, ordering costs should be determined or estimated for each inventory item in terms of dollars per order.

Carrying costs are the costs associated with holding items in inventory. They include storage or warehouse costs including rent, wages, utilities, insurance and so on. They also include the cost of the capital invested in the inventory and the cost of obsolescence, that is, the loss in value of the goods themselves if held too long. Obsolescence can also include physical deterioration of goods and loss of value due to changes in style as in the case of women's clothing, automobiles, etc. Carrying costs can be expressed as a percent of the total value of the inventory or as a dollar amount per unit per time period.

Finally, a third type of cost must also be considered. This is stock-out or shortage cost and refers to an inability to satisfy a demand for material because of a shortage. This may be an internal demand created by the production system or an external demand requiring delivery to a customer. In the case of internal demand, a stockout can in an extreme case cause production to cease entirely at a tremendous cost to the organization. If the demand comes from a customer, failure to deliver can result in loss of the sale, loss of future sales and loss of the customer's goodwill. Sometimes, as in the case of goodwill or loss of future sales, these costs are intangible and difficult to assess. However, they are costs and should be estimated as accurately as possible since they affect decisions which optimize inventory procedures. In discussing these procedures, we will stress ordering and carrying costs initially and then consider the effects of shortage costs later.

ACCOUNTING FOR INVENTORY

An inventory system is a set of procedures by which management reviews inventory levels on a periodic or continuous basis for the purpose of making inventory decisions. A small retailer might use a very informal system. He might simply scan his shelves and decide what and how much to order on a daily basis. Such a system might be called a periodic system in which case the review period is a single day.

A much more sophisticated system would be a continuous inventory system. In such a system the level of each item in inventory is monitored continuously. As items are added to or withdrawn from stock, the inventory level of that particular item is adjusted immediately. Such a system can be monitored manually or by computer. An example of a manual system might be a parts supply house in which items held in inventory for sale are stored in separate bins. A record card is attached to each bin with the total number of items in stock noted on the card. As parts are withdrawn from the bin, a notation is made on the card and the number removed is subtracted from the total. Of course, when a shipment of new parts is received and added to the inventory, the total is adjusted accordingly. In this way, the number of items of each kind that are in stock can be determined immediately by simply glancing at the card. Of course, such a system is extremely vulnerable to human error and the results are not always accurate. It is usually necessary to check such a system by taking an actual count on a periodic basis.

Computerized systems are more accurate and generally simpler to operate once they have been set up. Such systems are of two types: batch systems or real-time systems. A batch processing system is one in which additions and withdrawals are collected periodically and then used to update the inventory master file. In real-time systems, the master file is updated immediately as each transaction occurs. Batch and real-time computerized systems are analogous to periodic and continuous manual systems.

Regardless of the type of inventory accounting system in use, manual or computerized, batch or real time, decisions must be made regarding the number of items to hold in stock, the time at which orders should be placed, and the quantity to be ordered. In order to make these decisions in an optimal manner, the properties of the particular inventory system under consideration must first be identified and understood.

PROPERTIES OF AN INVENTORY SYSTEM

In attempting to determine the characteristics of a particular inventory system, it is necessary to consider four basic properties: demand, lead-time, costs, and other constraints. We will discuss each of these.

Demand

Before optimal inventory procedures can be established, it is necessary to make certain assumptions about the demand for the particular inventory item under consideration. Generally demand is expressed in terms of rate, that is, the number of units, or the quantity required per unit of time. Demand can be constant or variable. A constant demand is of course the easiest to deal with but unlikely in most situations. When a production schedule is based upon a contract that specifies a delivery schedule, the demand over the contractual period is or should be constant. This would not be so when the demand is market dependent. The demand for shoes experienced by the Butler Shoe Company or for room air conditioners manufactured by Westwind is uncertain and varies from period to period. And the demand for particular types or models of the product is even more variable than the demand for the product in general. In advanced inventory theory such demand, called *stochastic* or *probabilistic demand,* is dealt with using mathematical tools called *probability distributions.* However, this leads to unnecessary complexities, and frequently the resulting benefits are hardly worth the additional trouble. Even when demand is variable, satisfactory results, particularly for the small or medium-sized business, can often be obtained with simpler methods that utilize an estimated average demand. Furthermore, inaccuracies can result from the more complex methods if the wrong probability distribution is selected or if a suitable probability distribution cannot be found to represent the particular demand situation accurately. Managers must remember however that the average demand must be estimated for each inventory item to be controlled by the system.

Lead-time

Lead-time is the time that elapses between the placing of an order for goods or material and its receipt into inventory. As with demand, lead-time can be either constant or variable; however, it is most likely that lead-time varies from order to order even though the variability may be slight. Again, because of the complexities involved in dealing with probabilistic variables, average lead-time per item should be estimated and used as a constant value. If significant changes in lead-time do occur—the use of a new supplier might cause such a change—the model can be adjusted accordingly.

Costs

Although we have already discussed inventory costs, it appears worthwhile to mention them again here since they are also a property of the inventory system. The three types of costs that we must be concerned with are ordering costs, carrying costs, and shortage costs. A good accounting system should allow the first two types of costs to be determined with a reasonable degree of accuracy. Shortage costs are more difficult, if not impossible, to determine with precision and therefore must be estimated as closely as possible.

Other Constraints

Any physical system must operate under a set of constraints. The types of constraints on the system may vary, but they exist for any system. The most obvious constraint on an inventory system is that of space or capacity. Although quantity discounts may make it economical to order a thousand units of a particular item at a time, that order quantity becomes irrelevant if there is only enough space available to stock 500. Overall physical capacity may not be the only constraint on the system. Since many different items are usually held in inventory, an increase in the size of the inventory of one item may require a decrease in the size of the inventory of another. To optimize one may require a suboptimal decision about the other.

Working capital may also exercise a constraint on order quantities. The policy regarding stockouts or shortages could be another. In a critical production situation, management might decide that stockouts simply cannot be tolerated since their effect would be to disrupt the entire production system. On the other hand, in a retail or wholesale sales operation, stockouts may be acceptable; and back ordering, is a common practice.

ECONOMIC ORDER QUANTITY

The economic order quantity, or EOQ, answers the questions of how much to order at one time, how frequently to place orders, and when to place orders. The conditions necessary for determining the EOQ are that:

1. demand or average demand is constant, and
2. lead-time or average lead-time is constant.

Under these circumstances, the inventory of a particular item will behave much as the diagram in Figure 7.1 illustrates.

The economic order quantity is the maximum level that inventory will reach. As Figure 7.1 illustrates, we start with EOQ units in stock. Inventory declines at a constant rate according to the demand. When the inventory level reaches the reorder point, or ROP, an order is placed for an additional EOQ quantity. Inventory continues to decline during the lead-time but by the time the inventory level reaches

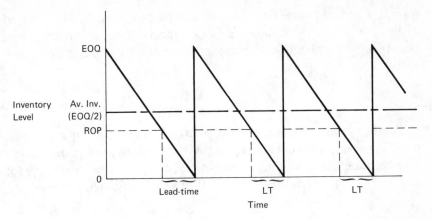

EOQ

Inventory Level

Av. Inv. (EOQ/2)

ROP

0

Lead-time   LT   LT

Time

Figure 7.1. Inventory behavior over time.

zero, the new order is received and the inventory level jumps to EOQ. This is a continuing process that goes on for as long as that particular item is stocked and used according to the established demand schedule. The determination of the EOQ and the ROP under the assumptions stated is quite simple.

In the basic EOQ model, the goal of management is to minimize the total inventory cost which in the simplest case consists only of ordering costs and carrying costs. To show how this is done, we will use the following symbols:

C_o represents ordering costs per order placed
C_c represents carrying cost per unit in inventory per year
D represents demand in units per year

As can be noted from Figure 7.1, the average quantity held in inventory over time is one-half the EOQ, or EOQ/2. The cost of carrying an inventory of a particular item is simply the carrying cost per unit multiplied by the average number of units carried,

$$C_c \times \frac{\text{EOQ}}{2}$$

An expression for the annual ordering cost can be determined in a similar manner. If D is the annual demand for the item and EOQ is the quantity ordered each time an order is placed, then the number of orders placed each year must be D/EOQ and the annual ordering cost is simply the number of orders placed multiplied by the cost per order,

$$\frac{D}{EOQ} \times C_O$$

Total costs are minimized at the point at which carrying costs equal ordering costs, that is, where these two expressions are equal. In order to determine EOQ, we simply equate the two expressions and solve for EOQ as follows with the multiplication sign eliminated:

$$\frac{D}{EOQ}C_O = C_c\frac{EOQ}{2}$$

$$2DC_O = (EOQ)^2 C_c$$

$$(EOQ)^2 = \frac{2DC_O}{C_c}$$

$$EOQ = \sqrt{\frac{2DC_O}{C_c}}$$

Westwinds, Inc.

One of the best revenue producers in Westwind's product line is their Model 350, 10,000 Btu room air conditioner. Westwind sells about 5000 of these units per year and expects demand for this unit, with some possible minor modifications, to remain at roughly the same level for several years.

Westwind purchases cabinets for its room air conditioners from the Excel Metal Company. In initiating a profit maximization program, Westwind management is reviewing its inventory procedures to determine what constitutes an optimal inventory policy. One phase of this review concerns the inventories of cabinets for each of its models.

Analysis of accounting records shows that ordering costs for cabinets are approximately $100 per order. The approximate annual unit cost of stocking cabinets is $4.00. Using the economic order quantity formula and substituting the numerical values, Westwind calculated EOQ as follows:

$$C_O = \$100.00$$

$$C_C = \$4.00$$

$$D = 5{,}000$$

therefore,

$$EOQ = \sqrt{\frac{2(5000)(\$100)}{\$400}} = 500$$

The economic order quantity for Model 350 cabinets is 500. Since the annual demand for that model is 5000 units, Westwind should place ten orders per year for 500 cabinets each. This answers the questions of how many should be ordered at one time and how frequently orders should be placed. It does not answer the question of when orders should be placed. In order to answer that, we must estimate the delivery lead-time required per order. Westwind's purchasing department examined their records of orders placed with Excel and estimated that the average lead-time was two weeks. That is, it takes two weeks from the placement of an order for cabinets until the order is received and placed in inventory.

Under this policy, Westwind's maximum inventory of Model 350 cabinets will be 500. With a constant average demand of 5000 units per year, the weekly demand will be 5000 divided by 50, (Westwind closes down for two weeks in August) or 100 per week. Since it takes two weeks from the placement of the order to the receipt of the cabinets, Westwind must place each order exactly two weeks before the inventory of cabinets reaches the zero point in order for no shortages to occur. At a depletion rate of 100 per week, this means that the order must be placed when the inventory level reaches 200.

The inventory policy for Model 350 cabinets can be summarized as follows. The EOQ is 500 units. Ten orders will be placed per year and the reorder point, or ROP, is 200. This policy minimizes the total cost of inventory, which in this case consists of carrying costs and ordering costs. Figure 7.2 illustrates the behavior of inventory under this policy.

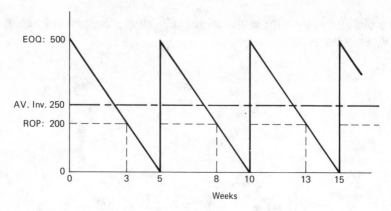

Figure 7.2. Inventory policy for Westwind Model 350 cabinet.

EOQ WITH QUANTITY DISCOUNTS

The inventory problem can become complicated by the common practice of price breaks or quantity discounts given by suppliers to encourage larger orders. The total costs incurred by the buyer include the cost of the merchandise purchased as well as the costs associated with ordering and carrying inventory. As long as the cost of the merchandise does not vary with the quantity ordered, it has no effect on the EOQ. Consequently, to this point we have only considered ordering and carrying costs in determining what the EOQ should be. However, if the price or cost of the merchandise depends on the quantity ordered, this must be taken into consideration in determining the optimal policy. When quantity discounts are a factor, the total cost associated with the purchase and stocking of a particular item is:

$$ \text{TC} = \frac{D}{\text{EOQ}} C_O + \frac{\text{EOQ}}{2} C_C + pD $$

In this formula, TC stands for total cost, p represents the per unit price of the item purchased and the other symbols are exactly the same as in the previous formulas.

When quantity discounts are possible, the previous formula for determining EOQ may no longer provide the lowest cost policy. Merely adding one unit to the order, for example, may reduce the unit price of the merchandise. The total cost would then be less than it would have been with the previously determined EOQ. Under these circumstances, the following procedure should be followed:

1. Determine the EOQ without considering the effect of quantity discounts as illustrated previously.
2. Calculate the total cost, *TC*, using that EOQ.
3. Calculate total cost at each price break quantity.
4. Select the order quantity that results in the lowest total cost.

This can be illustrated with the Westwind problem involving cabinets for the Model 350 room air conditioner that are purchased from the Excel Metal Company. The EOQ, ignoring quantity discounts was found to be 500. However, Excel, in order to encourage its customers to order in larger quantities, provided them with the following price schedule for cabinets:

QUANTITY	PRICE
under 1000	$7.90 each
1000 to 1499	$7.75 each
1500 to 1999	$7.60 each
2000 and over	$7.50 each

Given this price schedule, is 500 still the most economical order size?

The first step in determining the EOQ with quantity discounts is to compute the total cost using the previously determined EOQ. Recall that:

$$C_O = \$100.00$$
$$C_C = \$4.00$$
$$D = 5,000.$$

Then, when EOQ is 500, total cost is

$$TC = \frac{D}{EOQ}C_O + \frac{EOQ}{2}C_C + pD$$

and by substitution we get

$$TC = \left(\frac{5000}{500}\right)(\$100.00) + \left(\frac{500}{2}\right)(\$4.00) + (\$7.90)(5000)$$
$$= \$41,500.$$

The first price break occurs if Westwind increases the size of its orders to 1000 units. At that point, the unit price decreases to $7.75. We must now compute the total cost at a purchase quantity of 1000. In other words, using the total cost formula above we substitute 1000 for EOQ and $7.75 for p. The total cost now becomes:

$$TC = \left(\frac{5000}{1000}\right) (\$100.00) + \left(\frac{1000}{2}\right) (\$4.00) + (\$7.75)(5000)$$

$$= \$41,250.$$

Since total cost with an order quantity of 1000 is less than total cost with an order quantity of 500, the original EOQ of 500 is no longer the most economical under this price schedule. We still can't be sure that 1000 is the most economical order quantity until we check the total cost at the other price-break quantities. Using the same formula, at 1500 the total cost would be $41,333, and at 2000 the total cost would be $41,750. The minimum total cost occurs when the order quantity is 1000 units. Consequently the new EOQ with quantity discounts should be 1000, five orders will be placed each year and the reorder point is still 200 since there is no indication that the lead-time for the larger order is any longer than it was previously.

SAFETY STOCK

So far the development of an optimal inventory policy was based on the assumption that demand was a known and constant quantity or that the average demand could be treated as such. The first case is an oversimplification. Except in very unusual circumstances, demand is variable. When demand is interpreted and treated as the average demand over the period, departures from the optimal results will be minimized. Although there could be occasional shortages and occasional instances of excessive inventory, in the long run the results will approximate those of the optimal policy.

In the initial EOQ determination, when the inventory level of a particular item falls to a predetermined reorder point, an order is placed for that item in the calculated economic order quantity. The ROP is set to take into account the delivery lead-time so that if the normal usage of the item continues during the lead-time, the inventory level reaches zero just as the new order is received. But suppose the actual demand for the item deviates from the estimated average demand. Then inventory may reach the reorder point earlier or later than expected. This should create no problem since the ROP is based on the inventory level not on any specific date or time. However, if demand during the lead-time is greater than the average, inventory will reach the zero point before the new order arrives and a stockout occurs.

In many types of business, a stockout may not be serious or costly. The loss of the sale of a $30.00 pair of shoes once or twice a month is hardly critical to the success of the business. In various businesses, a product may be backordered for future delivery to the customer with no loss incurred. However, in many cases a stockout can be extremely costly, most obviously when a production line has to shut down because of a shortage of materials. Lost sales, particularly of large ticket items can be significant, especially to the small business. Consequently, in these types of situations, it may be advantageous to maintain a buffer or safety stock in inventory to guard against those times when demand during the lead-time period exceeds the average. In order to determine how much safety stock should be carried the cost of a stockout must be estimated.

Shortage or stockout cost, designated C_S, is crucial to safety stock determination. However, it is often impossible to estimate this cost with a great deal of accuracy or with a high degree of confidence. Many factors contribute to the cost of a shortage. For example, although a material shortage in a manufacturing operation may create a serious disruption and delay, measuring the cost is often difficult. Idle time of production workers, special handling costs, shutdown and start-up costs, may not be segregated in the accounting records. If a shortage results in a lost sale we can impute a cost to the lost transaction, but there can be no absolute certainty that the sale was actually lost due to the shortage. Furthermore, there is the loss of customer goodwill and loss of future sales which can never be accurately estimated. How do we determine the cost due to the loss of a valued customer?

For these and many other reasons, it may not be possible to estimate C_S with any great amount of precision. Nevertheless, without some estimate we would have to operate on the basis of the simplified model which assumes a fixed and constant demand and provides for no safety stock whatsoever.

Another problem with regard to safety stock is determining the likelihood or probability that the variable demand will assume different levels. In typical inventory problems, this determination requires the selection and application of a theoretical probability distribution to represent demand. This is an unnecessary complication, for the manager is unlikely to be conversant with the various concepts of probability theory and simply has no time to learn them on the job. This complication can be avoided if the manager makes subjective estimates, aided by whatever empirical evidence is available, of the probability that demand during lead-time will exceed average demand by certain amounts, say by 5%, 10%, and 15%. This can be done by the betting odds method described in the previous chapter or by using relative frequencies obtained from records of past demand during lead-time periods. This latter method will be illustrated in the following section. Having an estimated stockout cost and a set of probabilities, an optimal safety stock can be determined.

Safety Stock For Westwind

EOQ and ROP have already been determined for the Westwind Model 350 cabinet based on an assumed constant demand of 100 units per week. The concept of a known and constant demand is much more reasonable and likely for a manufacturing operation where demand at the production line can be scheduled than it would be for a retail store, for example, where demand is determined by the market and is beyond the control of management. However, even in manufacturing, the production schedule must be determined by demand to some degree. As the demand increases, production must also increase in order to keep pace and make deliveries. Consequently, Westwind's production manager decides that a safety stock of necessary parts and materials should be maintained in inventory in order to preclude shortages that could interrupt the production process.

Since the cabinet represents the last step in the production of the Model 350, a shortage of cabinets would delay shipment of the product and could back up and finally stop production. When such a shortage occurs, as it has in the past when no safety stock was maintained, a special order for cabinets had to be prepared and the order itself was given special handling. Delays in shipments have occasionally caused order cancellations and, as a result, the loss of customer goodwill from those customers affected. The cost of a shortage of cabinets is estimated at about $35.00 per unit short. Remember that inventory carrying costs for cabinets are $4.00 per unit. How large a safety stock of Model 350 cabinets should Westwind maintain?

In determining safety stock, the production manager must be primarily concerned with a change in demand that might occur during the two-week lead-time period from the placement of an order until it is delivered. From the previous example on EOQ for Westwind, the average demand during lead-time is for 200 cabinets. The production manager examined production records for the past two years and recorded the frequency with which demand exceeded the calculated average demand by 5%, 10%, 15% and more. The two years studied represent 100 weeks of production or 50 lead-time periods. When such records exist, it is possible to use the frequencies of past occurrences to estimate the probabilities of future occurrences. The results are as follows:

DEMAND	SHORTAGE	FREQUENCY	PERCENT	PROBABILITY
Average	0 units	35	70%	0.70
+ 5%	10 units	8	16%	0.16
+ 10%	20 units	5	10%	0.10
+ 15%	30 units	2	4%	0.04
		50	100%	1.00

The values in the probability column are obtained by simply dividing each frequency by 50 which is the sum of the frequencies. This provides a *relative frequency estimate* of the probability. The data indicate that in the past, with no safety stock, 70% of the time there were no shortages, 16% of the time were was a shortage of 10 units, 10% of the time there was a shortage of 20 units, and 5% of the time there was a shortage of 30 units. If the no-safety-stock policy is extended into the future, we can estimate that no shortage will occur with a probability of 0.7, a shortage of approximately 10 units will occur with a probability of 0.16, a shortage of 20 units will occur with a probability of 0.10, and a shortage of 30 units will occur with a probability of 0.04.

Given the set of costs (carrying costs, ordering costs, and shortage costs) and the set of probabilities, we can now determine the total cost of maintaining various levels of safety stock. We of course want to determine that policy for which total costs are a minimum. If we find that a safety stock of Q_S units should be carried, we will simply adjust the ROP so that if demand during the lead-time is average, the new order will arrive when exactly Q_S units remain in inventory.

Consider Westwind's EOQ before quantity discounts were introduced. The EOQ was 500 and the number of orders per year was 10. In determining the amount of safety stock to carry, the objective is to minimize the total additional inventory cost on an annual basis, that is, the total additional cost incurred by carrying different levels of safety stock, including a safety stock of zero. For example, the additional carrying cost is the carrying cost per unit per year multiplied by the number of units of safety stock carried.

The annual shortage or stockout cost is the unit cost of a stockout times the number of units short times the probability associated with the shortage times the number of orders placed per year. The last factor in the multiplication is necessary because the opportunity for a shortage occurs each time an order is placed. Remember that in Westwind's case the annual carrying cost per unit was $4.00, the stockout cost was estimated at $35.00 per unit, and the number of orders placed per year was 10. We will first determine the total additional cost to Westwind if no safety stock is carried, that is, if safety stock is zero. With zero safety stock there will be no additional carrying costs, and therefore, we simply determine the expected shortage cost as follows:

$$(\$35)(10)(0.16)(10) + (\$35)(20)(0.10)(10) + (\$35)(30)(0.04)(10)$$
$$= \$560 + \$700 + \$420$$
$$= \$1680.$$

With the same type of computation we can determine the expected cost due to stockouts if we maintain a safety stock of ten units. The per unit stockout cost and the number of orders per year are unchanged. Note that with a ten unit safety stock, if demand exceeds the average by 5% there will still be no shortage. If demand exceeds the average by 10% and 15% the shortages will be 10 and 20 units respectively with probabilities of 0.10 and 0.04. Consequently, the annual shortage costs with a safety stock of ten units is:

$$(\$35)(10)(0.10)(10) + (\$35)(20)(0.04)(10)$$
$$= \$350 + \$280$$
$$= \$630.$$

However, since an additional 10 units are carried in inventory for the year, we must add the additional carrying costs incurred. Since annual carrying costs per unit are $4.00, the total additional carrying costs are 10 times $4.00 or $40, and therefore, the total costs resulting from carrying a safety stock of 10 are $630 + $40 = $670. It should be obvious so far that since the cost with 10 units of safety stock is less than the cost with no safety stock, the former is preferable. However, we must still determine the costs with safety stocks of 20 and 30 units. These calculations are:

20 unit safety stock

Shortage cost: ($35)(10)(0.04)(10) = $140.

Additional carrying cost: ($4.00)(20) = $80.

Total cost: $140 + $80 = $220.

30 unit safety stock

Shortage cost: none, since according to the probability table determined previously, demand never exceeds + 15%.

Additional carrying cost: ($4.00)(30) = $120.

Total cost: $120.

Choosing the safety stock policy that results in the minimum cost obviously leads to a safety stock of 30 units. In order to do this, the original ROP of 200 is changed to 230. This means, that each time the inventory of cabinets declines to 230 a new order is placed. If demand continues at the average level during lead-time, the new order will be received when there are still 30 cabinets remaining in inventory. However, if demand during lead-time increases by as much as 15%, there will be no shortage.

In this particular case, the optimal policy is to permit no shortages. This is due to the great difference between the cost of carrying one additional unit in inventory, $4.00, and the cost of being short one unit, $35.00. Obviously, it is much less costly to carry safety stock than it is to permit a shortage to occur. This is not necessarily the case. Suppose that carrying cost per unit was $40.00 instead of $4.00. The optimal policy is likely to be quite a bit different. We can determine the optimal policy by computing the costs for each level of safety stock as before using the new value for unit carrying cost. These costs would now be:

Zero safety stock: $1680
10 unit safety stock: $750
20 unit safety stock: $940
30 unit safety stock: $1200

In this case, the optimal policy would be to carry a safety stock of only 10 units. Beyond that, the carrying costs of additional inventory begin to outweigh the shortage costs. In order to keep a safety stock of 10 units, the ROP is adjusted to 210.

MATERIAL REQUIREMENTS PLANNING

A relatively recent concept that has gained widespread acceptance is that of material requirements planning, generally abbreviated MRP. The inventory methods discussed previously are extremely useful and effective in cases with independent demand for various inventory items, that is, when the demand for one particular item is unrelated to the demand for other items. This is not to say that these methods cannot be used or are ineffective in cases of dependent demand but simply that a comprehensive MRP system would be more efficient in such cases. Generally, the MRP system becomes most efficient in situations where the size and complexity of the inventory system is such that the simpler methods described here become difficult to apply. However, when MRP appears appropriate its implementation is quite complex and requires a computerized system. For that reason, we will not provide a detailed analysis of MRP but instead give a general description.

MRP applies to dependent demand inventory items. This means that the demand for a particular item depends upon the demand for some other item or product. This approach is particularly applicable in manufacturing operations where the demand for components and raw materials is dependent upon the demand for the end product.

MRP is a method for determining when to place orders for dependent demand items and how to reschedule and adjust for changes in demand estimates. The MRP system consists of inventory records, bills of materials, and computer programs that translate master production schedules into a time-phased net requirements plan for each item required. MRP avoids the averaging process that was used in the previously described inventory procedures. The essential feature and primary advantage of MRP is that it calculates the specific quantity required of each component or material and determines precisely when orders should be placed.

The benefits of MRP are similar to the benefits derived from any inventory system that tends to optimize inventory and ordering procedures. These benefits include smaller inventories, reduced idle time, reduced shortages, better customer service and so on. The greatest cost of the MRP system is the cost of purchasing or leasing a computer system with the capacity to support the function. The system also requires trained personnel with expertise in the MRP concept as well as computer specialists to interact with the system. However, MRP software is usually provided, at some cost, by the computer manufacturers.

Although originally intended for manufacturing operations, MRP can be applied to other types of business. However, for the small or medium-sized business, a thorough cost analysis should be conducted to determine if the benefits of MRP are sufficiently greater than those of the simple inventory systems described here to justify its cost.

SUMMARY

Inventories of products, supplies and materials are essential to almost every type of business operation. They can however be one of the major causes of profit erosion in the business. Excessive inventories, shortages, special orders and so on create costs that could be avoided by properly applying methods for optimizing the inventory system. The goal of these procedures is to minimize the total cost of maintaining inventories. These total costs are actually the sum of several different costs, i.e., inventory carrying costs, ordering costs and shortage costs. Frequently, the reduction of one type of cost results in an increase in another.

The determination of an optimal inventory policy requires finding economic order quantities, reorder points and safety stock levels under varying demand conditions and different vendor pricing policies.

In very complex, demand-dependent situations, a computerized MRP system could be advantageous. However, for the small or medium-sized business, a cost-benefit analysis should be conducted to determine if the benefits of such a system would outweigh the costs involved. Frequently, the simpler methods described here are more beneficial to the small or medium-sized business.

8. Efficient Purchasing

No organizational function gets less attention from management experts than purchasing. With the exception of retailing, where the "buyer" is generally the first level line executive, purchasing is generally relegated to a sort of limbo receiving little recognition for good performance. However, when things go wrong, whether or not the fault of purchasing, it frequently gets the blame. In other words, management tends to ignore the purchasing function unless attention is called to it by adverse circumstances. This is an unfortunate situation because, in terms of profit maximization, purchasing is a key function. In fact, in only one kind of business can purchasing be relegated to a position of secondary importance, and that is a pure service business where the only purchased materials are supplies.

On the average, approximately 50% of every dollar expended is spent on the purchase of goods and services in manufacturing industries. In nonmanufacturing, this percentage can go as high as 80% or 85%. Consequently, a small reduction in the cost of purchasing can result in a sizable increase in the organization's profits. An analysis of cost of goods sold can determine the contribution that purchased materials make to overall costs. It is a simple analysis to make and by extension it is possible to determine the effect of a 5% or 10% decrease in purchasing costs on the profit and loss picture of the firm. Such an analysis should be an important part of the profit maximization program for any small or medium-sized business.

To illustrate the leverage that purchasing has on costs, consider a small manufacturer with annual sales of a million dollars. The sales-cost-profit relationships are as follows:

Sales		$1,000,000
Purchased Material	$500,000	
Labor	300,000	
Overhead	150,000	
Total Costs		950,000
Profit		$ 50,000

Let's see what effect a 5% reduction in each cost category would have on total costs and profit for this organization.

A 5% decrease in overhead will lower total costs by only $7,500 and would increase profit by 15%.

A 5% decrease in labor costs lowers total costs by $15,000 and increases profit by 30%.

However, a 5% decrease in the cost of purchased materials lowers total costs by $25,000 and increases profit by 50%.

If these cost relationships stay the same, it is easy to see that it would be necessary to increase sales by 50% in order to increase profits by the same 50% that could be accomplished by a 5% decrease in the cost of purchased materials. In the interest of efficiency, management should address itself to answering the question: Is it easier or more feasible to achieve a 50% increase in sales or to reduce the cost of purchased material by 5%? The answer is not as obvious as it seems and most likely must be obtained by a thorough analysis of both the sales and purchasing operations. However, in the context of profit maximization, such an analysis is always worthwhile.

In the following pages, we will discuss purchasing in the context of a manufacturing organization. However, the objectives and the functions performed are similar regardless of the type of business involved. The difference in purchasing or acquiring materials for input to a manufacturing process and in purchasing goods for resale is not in the purchasing procedures themselves but rather in the stage of production in which the goods are to be utilized. Raw materials must be processed through all stages of production before they can be marketed. Finished goods are already in their final stage and are ready for sale to the customer. In the material to follow we will constantly be referring to the *purchasing department* even though in some small businesses the department may consist of a single individual.

THE OBJECTIVES OF THE PURCHASING FUNCTION

The purchasing or procurement function has the responsibility for acquiring all products, materials and external services required for the operation of the business. The primary objective of purchasing should be to achieve the acquisition of these items in the most efficient manner possible. Efficiency in purchasing should be considered in relation to several characteristics of the procured item. These characteristics are:

1. The type, quantity and quality required—that is, the material procured must be the material required in every respect;
2. The place and time of delivery—the materials must be available when and where needed;
3. The purchase price.

It is interesting to note that although the purchasing department must concern itself with each of these factors, it actually has no control over any of them. Factors 1 and 2 are determined by the users of the material or products within the organization and transmitted to the purchasing department on a purchase requisition form. The price is determined by the vendor but is of course subject to negotiation. If alternative sources for the product or material exist, the purchasing department can exert some influence over the price charged by negotiating, by requiring competitive bidding, or simply by shopping.

In terms of the most efficient performance of purchasing, the goal of the department should be to assure that the required materials are provided at the time and place needed by a reliable vendor and at the lowest price possible. In achieving this goal certain functions must be performed. These include:

1. Receipt and handling of purchase requisitions
2. Issuance of purchase orders
3. Selection of vendors
4. Maintenance of vendor files
5. Maintenance of purchasing files and records

6. Follow-up
7. Contract negotiation and administration

These functions will be discussed in connection with the topics that follow.

PURCHASING IN THE ORGANIZATIONAL STRUCTURE

There is no single best place for the purchasing department in the organization. Its position will vary depending on the size of the organization, the type of organization and the relative importance of the purchasing function in the context of the overall operation of the business. For example, as previously stated, purchasing in a service business will not have the same importance or status it would have in a manufacturing operation.

In a very small business, purchasing may be a one man job or even the part-time job of someone with other responsibilities. Even in somewhat larger organizations, the purchasing function can often be split among several different individuals. For example, the office manager in a small company might want to have the responsibility for the purchase of all office supplies. The manager may then delegate this function to one of his subordinates as a full-time or part-time responsibility. Within the same organization, the supervisor of building maintenance might retain the responsibility for purchasing supplies associated with that function. However, if this happens to be a manufacturing operation, the purchasing of materials for the manufacturing process is the responsibility of a purchasing department which reports to the head of production.

The splitting of purchasing responsibilities may be expedient in a small company; however, as the volume of purchases increases, a centralized purchasing department is generally much more efficient. The procurement of all externally supplied items by a single, centralized department leads to more efficient and economical operations. A centralized purchasing department handles all procurement activities under the authority of a specialist who devotes his entire attention to procurement for the entire firm and relieves individual department heads or managers of that additional responsibility. This eliminates duplication of effort and allows line managers to devote their attention to their primary responsibilities.

The purchasing operation itself becomes more efficient because all of the purchasing records are centralized, all orders emanate from the same source providing easier follow-up, and purchases can be made in larger quantities frequently leading to savings through quantity discounts. In general, when the value of purchases increases to the point where the full-time activities of a single individual are warranted, a separate, centralized purchasing department should be established.

Westwind, Inc.

Westwind, Inc., a manufacturer of ventilating fans and room air conditioners, is a medium-sized company. The bulk of Westwind's procurement activities involves the purchase of component parts and materials for its manufacturing operation. Because of the size of the company, the volume of the purchases made and the nature of those purchases, the purchasing function has been centralized and a purchasing department for the company has been established. The director of purchasing reports directly to the vice-president in charge of production.

For a short time after the purchasing department was established, office and other types of supplies continued to be purchased by the heads of various departments on an as needed basis. However, it soon became apparent that greater efficiency and economy could be achieved if all purchases were made by the central department. Consequently, purchases of all types including supplies became the responsibility of the central purchasing department. This has not only relieved department heads of this task allowing them to devote additional time to their other duties, but it has also avoided overpurchasing of certain items due to duplicate purchase orders being written by several departments for the same product or material. At the same time, economies have been affected due to fewer orders of larger quantities. This has allowed Westwind to benefit from quantity discounts when previously numerous small orders were often placed for the same item.

The Butler Shoe Company

The Butler Shoe Company falls into the category of a small retail business. As described in a previous chapter, the company operates three retail stores. When George Butler started the original store in 1948, he performed all of the management functions himself, including purchasing. When the two suburban stores were opened in 1955 and 1960, purchasing for each store became the responsibility of the store managers. However, it soon became apparent that there was much duplication of effort including several purchase orders for exactly the same merchandise. Also, placing and following up on the orders was consuming a great deal of the time of each manager that could have been more profitably devoted to selling, merchandising and generally running the store. George Butler decided to centralize all purchasing activities in the downtown store. The central department was established to handle purchases of merchandise for resale and supplies for all of the stores. The department consists of one individual and a secretary who devote full time to the purchasing function. Although, at first, expenses appeared to increase, these were soon more than offset by lower purchasing costs, greater efficiency and a considerable decrease in the aggravation level of the store managers.

Tech-Ed Schools, Inc.

The Tech-Ed Schools organization chart appears in Chapter 3. Being a proprietary business and technical school providing a service rather than a product, purchases are limited to supplies and various educational materials sold to students in the book store operated by Tech-Ed. The purchasing function is the responsibility of the Administration Department along with other administrative functions. These functions tend to become departmentalized as the volume and value of the work associated with each one increases to the point where the full-time attention of at least one individual is required. At the present time, purchasing is the responsibility of a single individual who reports directly to the administrative vice-president.

PURCHASING INTERFACES

Because of the nature of the purchasing function, the purchasing department interfaces with practically every other department within the organization. In a sense, purchasing is a service function. Its primary goal is to meet the requirements of other departments in terms of the materials needed in order for them to perform their functions. One measure of how well a purchasing department performs its function is the degree of satisfaction or dissatisfaction that other departments experience with respect to how well their requirements are filled.

When an inventory control system is operating, most purchase requisitions will originate in the warehouse or stores section of the organization from the individual in charge of inventories. The purchase requisition will note the quantity to be ordered and the date that delivery is required. Although one of the responsibilities of purchasing is to attempt to procure the required materials at the lowest possible price, purchasing does not have the authority to change the quantity ordered so as to take advantage of quantity discounts. If optimal inventory policies are used, as discussed in the previous chapter, the quantity ordered will be the EOQ which takes quantity discounts into consideration. If an especially advantageous price break can be achieved based on quantities that did not enter into the EOQ determination previously, then it is the responsibility of purchasing to provide this new information to inventory control so that a new EOQ can be determined. Purchasing must not make any changes to the purchase requisition without first consulting the originator.

In placing orders with vendors, the purchasing department must also abide by the material specifications prepared by the engineering department or other originators of the purchase requisition. Frequently in developing specifications, engineers consider only the technical requirements of the application without regard to cost. Sometimes the quality specified is much higher than that which is actually required. Coordination between engineering and purchasing can often make the engineering department aware of the cost aspect of the purchase and can sometimes get them to modify their specifications when they are more stringent than necessary. This too can often lead to large savings for the firm. Experience has shown that there are many instances when materials of somewhat lower quality can be substituted without affecting the end product or result. Of course, this can only be done with the concurrence of the engineering department.

Regardless of the type of business, purchase requisitions can originate from many diverse areas within the organization. They can come from maintenance personnel, office managers, warehouse or stores managers, and so on. Consequently, close coordination between the purchasing department and all of the requesting departments is essential if purchasing costs are to be minimized. By keeping the requestors informed about prices, the quality of materials, the status of orders, etc., costs can be minimized and purchasing efficiency enhanced.

PURCHASING INPUTS

To a large extent, the efficiency of the purchasing department is dependent upon the inputs it receives from other departments. Being essentially a service operation, the service it provides depends upon the information it receives. For example, it is difficult for purchasing to procure a particular part that is required in manufacturing if the part is poorly or vaguely specified. Requests for purchasing to acquire some needed material are submitted in the form of a *purchase requisition*.

There is no standard purchase requisition form that we can describe here since most organizations design their own. However, there are certain items of information that should be included on every purchase requisition. These are:

1. An identifying number
2. The name and department of the originator
3. The date of submittal
4. A detailed description of the material to be ordered
5. The quantity of the material required
6. The date that delivery is required
7. The name and number of the account to be charged
8. Any additional information that would assist the purchasing department in procuring the material

All of the above listed items are supplied by the requestor. The following items should be filled in by the purchasing department:

1. The purchase order number
2. The date the purchase order is submitted
3. The name of the vendor
4. The name of the buyer
5. Shipping instructions

When the purchase requisition originates in the warehouse as a result of the inventory control procedure for recurring requirements and standard parts and materials, it is not necessary to prepare a new purchase requisition every time an item is ordered. In cases of recurring demand, a *traveling purchase requisition* is often used. This is simply a card that is maintained for each item kept in inventory. The card contains information on the item required, the order quantity, a description of the item, possible vendors or suppliers and so on. When the stock level in inventory drops to the reorder point, the card is sent to the purchasing department and a purchase order is prepared from the information on the card. Of course, computerized systems may use somewhat different procedures, but the underlying theory is the same.

A *bill of materials* is a list of all of the items needed to produce a particular product. The bill of materials is prepared from the engineering drawings. From the bill of materials and the production schedule, the purchasing department can determine in advance the types and quantities of the materials needed and the times at which they are required. When this information is sent to purchasing, the necessity for preparing individual purchase requisitions for each production item is eliminated thus saving a great deal of time and effort on the part of the purchasing department. This procedure is of course primarily applicable to the procurement of standard items.

Sometimes a detailed description of the item required is necessary. Such a description is called a *specification*. A product specification can accompany the purchase requisition and can also be sent to the vendor along with the purchase order to assure compliance. There are several types of specifications including blueprints or engineering drawings, market grades, commercial standards, material specifications, performance specifications and so on.

If a product cannot be described adequately by a single type of specification, then several can be used. For example, a blueprint, a material specification and a performance specification could all accompany a particular purchase requisition. The more information available to the purchasing department about the requirements of the originator, the better it will be able to provide its service to the satisfaction of the requesting department.

PURCHASING PROCEDURES

It is probably stating the obvious to call attention to the fact that businesses vary as to size, function (that is wholesaling, retailing, manufacturing, etc.), industry, and so on. Purchasing procedures will of course differ among different types of businesses. They will also differ depending upon the type of product to be purchased and the quantity and frequency of the purchases. In general however four broad categories of purchasing requirements can be identified. These are:

1. Continuous use items ordered periodically
2. Large value items ordered as required
3. Small value items ordered periodically
4. Normal purchases

Of course, as with most classification systems, these categories are somewhat arbitrary and in some cases might overlap. Some other set of classifications might serve just as well to categorize the various types of purchases and purchasing procedures; however, these appear to be adequate and serve the purpose quite well. We will consider each category separately.

Continuous Use Items

Items that are used continuously and for which there is a reasonably predictable demand can usually be purchased under a *blanket purchase order*. Blanket, or open-ended, purchase orders allow the purchase requisition to be sent directly to the supplier and bypass the purchasing department. This eliminates the necessity for writing an individual purchase order each time some particular item has to be reordered. Initially, the purchasing department negotiates a contract for a fixed time period. If the contract does not specify the price because the time period involved is of such a length that a price change could occur during the term of the contract, the price for any shipment would be the standard price that is in effect at the time when a particular shipment is ordered. When blanket purchase orders are used, the releasing of purchase orders during the period for which the blanket order was negotiated becomes a routine matter resulting in significant savings in the purchasing function.

Large Value Items

Purchases of large value items generally involve such things as machinery, computers, vehicles and other capital goods that are purchased only once at infrequent intervals as the need arises. Purchases of such items are sometimes characterized as *purchase by requirement*. This is because the purchasing activity for such items is initiated to satisfy a requirement only at the time that the need is recognized.

When such an item is needed for a specific purpose and if time is not a problem, bids are often called for. When time is an important factor, the purchasing department may solicit a vendor from a list of approved suppliers to provide the required item. Competitive bidding is not involved in such a case. In either case, whether competitive bidding is called for or not, as much planning and evaluation of the purchase and the potential supplier should be performed prior to the purchase decision considering the time constraints involved, the value of the equipment to be purchased and the volume of the order. Price, though a major factor in such purchases, should not be the only determinant. Product capability, quality, reputation of the vendor and the promised delivery date all represent important items that should be factored into the decision process.

Small Value Items

Low cost items used infrequently but with some regularity fall into this category. Sometimes the cost of performing the normal purchasing procedures exceeds the cost of the items purchased in this category. In that case, it is often advantageous to purchase these items out of petty cash accounts or by using blanket or open-ended purchase requisitions. In such a case, the purchasing department does not do the actual purchasing but simply establishes the conditions to be adhered to and monitors the system. Purchasing small value items in this manner can often result in significant savings for the business.

Normal Purchases

Any items purchased that do not fall into one of the above three categories are lumped into the category of normal purchases. These purchases are handled by the normal procedures already described previously, that is, the issuance of a purchase requisition by the requesting department together with a bill of materials, a specification and any other data necessary to describe the required item. The purchasing department then follows its usual procedures in selecting the vendor, negotiating the contract, issuing the purchase order and so on. The purchasing department also coordinates the total procurement activity beginning with its receipt of the purchase requisition up to the delivery of the order.

SELECTION OF VENDORS

One of the principal responsibilities of any purchasing department is the screening and selection of vendors. Whenever a supplier must be chosen to provide a particular item, the purchasing department must attempt to locate vendors who can meet the requirements of the company in terms of the quantities required, the quality of the merchandise, the delivery date when the material is needed and the lowest possible cost. These requirements regarding quantity, quality, timing and cost are not necessarily consistent with one another and frequently some compromises must be made. For example, the lowest cost might require larger quantities than are needed at the time the order is placed. Or, the company that can provide the earliest delivery date might not have the highest quality product or the lowest cost.

The starting point in the vendor selection process is to compile a list of companies that can supply each required item. Then the relative rating of each potential vendor should be assessed. Some sort of a point scale can be developed for each pertinent characteristic of the vendor as well as a weighting system that takes into consideration the relative importance of the characteristics being evaluated. Sometimes the rating of vendors is made easier by actual visits to their plants or places of business. Other information about each potential vendor might be obtained from catalogs, price lists, data on previous experience with the vendor, etc. Of course, all such rating systems are highly subjective with the exception of ratings based on such hard data as prices. If Vendor A is consistently offering merchandise of comparable quality and at a lower price than Vendor B, he should no doubt be given a higher rating, that is, unless he has other drawbacks such as being able to supply only limited quantities or has a reputation for late deliveries, and so on. In the final analysis, the judgment of the purchasing agent is the most important ingredient in the rating and selection of vendors. When a numerical rating scale is used, the values assigned should be used only to order or rank the vendors from most preferred to least preferred. The actual numerical values assigned, being subject to personal opinion in their assessment, should largely be ignored otherwise.

Of course, the list of qualified vendors in order of preference only includes those vendor organizations acceptable to the purchasing organization in terms of the established standards. No vendor should be included on the list who is unacceptable for any reason whatsoever.

When a purchase requisition is issued, the purchasing department can then select a few vendors from the top of the list and contact each one. The final selection would then be based on their price quotations and delivery times. With every purchase, additional information is acquired and the original list can be revised when necessary. However, a decision should not be made on past data alone. It would be imprudent to purchase from the first name on the list without contacting several of the other approved vendors. Conditions change and the vendor that heads the list today may not be the best supplier tomorrow.

CONTROL OF QUALITY

Price is not the only criterion to be used in evaluating vendors. In fact, it is not even the most important. The most important criterion should be that of product quality. The lowest priced supplier may turn out to be the most expensive if he delivers material of poor or substandard quality. Production delays, scrap and waste, customer complaints, all resulting from the use and delivery of poor quality product can be quite costly to the company.

When quality is an important factor, the purchasing department should be the primary source of information regarding the quality of the product or service provided by each approved vendor. Although final decisions regarding the quality of any incoming material must be made by the user or the quality control or inspection department, information provided by purchasing can be instrumental in making that decision. Furthermore, information about product quality obtained either through usage or through inspection or testing by the quality control department should be fed back to the purchasing department for inclusion in their records and used for future purchasing decisions.

Inspection of incoming material is generally the responsibility of the quality control department. The purpose of incoming inspection is to verify that the supplier is delivering items that will meet the contractual specifications. There is no point in purchasing to specification if no provision is made to determine compliance. Inspection can be on a 100% basis or on a sampling basis called sampling inspection. Details of quality control procedures will be covered in Chapter 10 which is devoted to that subject.

MAKE OR BUY

The make or buy decision is of course limited to organizations involved in manufacturing. For such companies, there are frequent situations in which a decision must be made to either purchase a required item or to manufacture it for their own use. When a make or buy decision is appropriate, the purchasing and engineering departments must cooperate in making that decision.

In the course of making the make or buy decision, the relative merits of each course of action must be weighed. Cost, quality, delivery and so on are all involved. In fact, make or buy is similar to the process involved in selecting between alternate vendors. Purchasing must interact closely with the engineers and technicians who design the parts and products which are the subject of the decision. When engineering completes the design of a part, it issues an engineering release complete with a bill of materials or parts list, and instructions about the part such as where it is used, a part number, and manufacturing and service information. The engineering release can initiate a decision process which determines whether to purchase that part or to manufacture it in-house. If the company lacks the technology or the capacity to manufacture the part, then there is no decision to be made. In that case, the part must be purchased from an outside supplier. However, a firm that has the in-house capability must consider the make or buy decision.

Frequently, the make or buy decision is made by a committee of representatives from manufacturing, engineering and purchasing. Or, in some cases, the chief executive of the company may make the decision based on information he receives from these departments. The greater the amount of money involved, the more time and effort should be devoted to the decision process.

The purchasing input to the decision includes cost information about potential suppliers. In order to obtain up-to-date and timely information, bids may be solicited. Costs associated with manufacturing should be provided by the representatives of the manufacturing department based on past experience with similar products. The accounting department can supply information about indirect costs.

With the information regarding the costs of both alternatives, the appropriate managers can make or recommend what the decision should be. Obviously, the decision should favor the least cost alternative when all pertinent costs are considered.

THE PURCHASING INFORMATION SYSTEM

The purchasing information system is a system of records that provides a history of past purchasing activities as well as the present status of purchase orders in process. Since purchasing is a repetitive process, accurate records are necessary for its efficient operation. Although the establishment and maintenance of a good information system has a cost associated with it, the savings derived in the form of a more efficient and effective operation more than offset these costs.

Most purchasing departments maintain the following basic records:

1. Purchase order log
2. Open order file
3. Closed order file
4. Vendor records
5. Commodity records
6. Contract file

The *purchase order log* contains a numerical record of all purchase orders issued. The log usually contains the purchase order number, the name of the vendor, a description of the material ordered, and the amount of the order.

The *open order file* provides the status of all outstanding orders. Each file contains the purchase requisition, a copy of the purchase order, and any contracts and correspondence pertaining to the order. The *closed order file* is an historical record of all completed purchases.

The *vendor record* provides information about suppliers. A separate file is kept on each supplier. In addition to the supplier's name and address, phone number, name of contacts, etc., information about the supplier's performance, the quality of his product, capabilities, etc. can also be added.

A *commodity record* is maintained on major products, materials, and services that are purchased frequently. This record consists of a card or sheet or folder on each commodity showing the orders placed, receipts, and disbursements. The *contract file* contains special items that are not procured by a regular purchase order.

In small companies, the purchasing information system is often a paper system. However, with the increased accessibility of computers through time sharing or small, desk top systems which are low enough in cost to be within the reach of even very small businesses, much or all of the data in the system can be computerized. A computerized information system does not change the functions of the purchasing department but simply provides quicker access and more accurate and current information.

DETERMINING THE EFFICIENCY OF THE PURCHASING DEPARTMENT

Management must always be concerned with the efficiency of any operation but particularly with the purchasing operation because of the large amounts of expenditures for which it is responsible. An efficient purchasing department can save money and improve profits. An inefficient operation can be a major source of profit erosion. Consequently, some periodic effort at evaluating purchasing performance is worthwhile particularly as part of a profit maximization program.

Various criteria can be established for such an evaluation. Comparison of average prices paid for commodities purchased with average market prices can indicate if purchasing is saving money by the appropriate selection of vendors, use of quantity discounts and effective negotiation. Functional efficiency can be evaluated by determining the frequency of late deliveries or of purchase order errors.

Frequently attempts are made to evaluate the performance of the purchasing department by using various indexes such as the cost per purchase order issued or the cost of buying. The latter is determined by dividing the operating expenses of the purchasing department by the total value of its purchases. However, such indexes can be misleading. The cost of buying ratio can be low if little effort is made to secure materials at low prices. Therefore, the value of purchases is large compared to the operating expenses of the department. Rather than indicating higher efficiency, it can mean poor performance.

Evaluation of the department should be based on a careful analysis of its performance over a sufficient period of time to justify the results obtained and should examine all aspects of its operation. If performance indexes are used then several should be used because no single index taken alone can measure performance efficiency.

SUMMARY

The importance of the purchasing function in many organizations is often underrated. Yet it is perhaps one of the most important business functions with respect to profit maximization. Inefficient purchasing can lead to profit erosion through overpayment for goods and services, through the purchase of poor quality merchandise, and through delays and excessive costs resulting from late delivery of required materials.

On the other hand, an efficient purchasing operation backed up by an effective purchasing information system is an extremely valuable asset. Because purchasing efficiency cannot usually be expressed in simple quantitative terms, a thorough evaluation of all aspects of the purchasing function is essential to the success of the profit maximization program.

9. Controlling Production

Every business organization is a production system. We stated this fact early in the book and believe that it bears repeating here. A production system consists of inputs, a process and outputs. The outputs are of course the product or service provided by the organization. The inputs to the system vary depending upon the type of organization but can include labor, materials, information, equipment, supervision and so on. The process refers to those activities or functions which convert the inputs into the desired outputs.

It should be obvious that a production system must be controlled. Control is one of the basic functions of the manager. So the question is not, "Should there be a production control system?" but "What kind of system should there be and how should it work?"

In a sense the topics already discussed in previous chapters are part of the larger production control system. Cost, volume and breakeven analysis provide information regarding the optimum levels of production in terms of profit, a necessary input to any profit maximization program. Planning production capacity and optimizing inventories are also a part of the control system. However, at this point we must be primarily concerned with the production process itself. Of course there is more than one kind of production system, and techniques suitable for one type may not be suitable for some other. We will consider here the control problems associated with the three basic types of production systems: continuous production systems, intermittent production systems and service systems. The first two are manufacturing systems while the third refers to nonmanufacturing operations. We will initially consider the manufacturing systems.

A manufacturing organization tries to produce the right quantity and quality of product at the least cost and at the time desired by the customer. Production control is a management technique which attempts to gain the best utilization of the company's resources and facilities. This is done by the integration and coordination of materials, machines, and manpower employed in the manufacturing cycle. Production control therefore focuses its attention on work-in-process, that is, the transformation of materials into the finished products requested by customers.

Production control includes two major aspects. The first aspect pertains to the total volume of production for a month, quarter or other period of time. An estimate of the total volume is necessary in order to make plans for purchasing raw materials, employing and training workers, financing the program, and for other general areas. This is related to capacity planning as discussed previously.

The second aspect of production control concerns the planning and controlling of detailed operations from week to week or day to day. This planning provides for the production of goods to meet the requirements of individual customers or for the production of specific items for inventory. The detailed production plan prescribes size, color, or other detailed specifications; indicates the number of items to be produced and provides for the operations carried out at each workplace or machine. This second aspect or phase of production control can be broken down into several steps. First, plans are made for the work to be done. This activity is generally called *routing*. Then a schedule is established for determining when each operation will be started and completed. As one would expect, this step is called *scheduling*. Next, the plans are put into effect by issuing directions for carrying out the various steps in the plan. This is called *dispatching* because it involves issuing orders to the persons who do the work. Finally, the work is reviewed to determine if and how well it has been accomplished and to revise the plan if necessary. This last step is referred to as *follow-up*.

Each step in production control includes certain activities peculiar to this activity. Routing includes plans for the machine or the workplace where the work will be done, the type of manufacturing operations to be performed, and the quantity that will be produced. It indicates the method by which the product will be made and prescribes the operations for making each part and each subassembly. Routing also includes the determination of the order in which the work will be done. Finally, routing includes determining where the work will be done. The departments expected to do the work and also the machines in each department may be specified. In short, routing includes all the preliminary planning up to the point where the time schedules are established.

Scheduling fixes the time when the work will be done, that is, the date of completion or delivery to customers. Starting dates and dates of transfer from one department to another may be decided upon in order that completion dates can be met.

Dispatching means the execution of the plans as established by routing and scheduling. It includes the preliminary work of preparation prior to the starting date as well as the issuance of orders to the manufacturing departments. Before the factory begins work on the product, materials may be purchased, machines may be repaired or set up for the work, workers may be employed or trained, and machine tools may be manufactured or purchased. When work is started, orders and instructions are issued to workers and to various departments including the storeroom, materials handling and inspection.

Follow-up includes checking up on the work as it progresses, comparing the progress with the original plans, and taking such corrective action as may be necessary or possible.

The details of the steps in the production control process will vary with the company, the product, and the persons responsible for the planning.

While production control is necessary in all manufacturing, the extent of its use will vary with the different types of operations. Its use is minimal in a company which manufactures one standard product on a repetitive basis and sells to its customers from finished stock. Once the production process has been established little additional planning and control are necessary. Material in production automatically proceeds from one operation to the next along a balanced production line until the product is completed. The production planning and control which precede the start of manufacturing remain the same as long as there are no changes in the product or process. At the other extreme, there is job lot production which manufactures a number of different products only on the receipt of orders. The process layout in that case needs much prior planning.

Without exception, every order should be subjected to the planning and control process to achieve management's objectives. While these two types of production represent the extremes, there are many variations of manufacturing systems in between. The complexity of the production control system will vary accordingly. As manufacturing approaches a repetitive operation, the problem is simplified; increased diversity of production will make for a more complicated procedure.

THE PLACE OF PRODUCTION CONTROL IN THE ORGANIZATION

The place of the production control department in an organization is not rigid. It depends upon the importance which management assigns to this activity. Usually this department is under the factory or production manager who is responsible for the operations of the line departments and all production staff activities.

The work of the production control department forms the basis for decisions by a number of other company departments. Likewise, production control cannot initiate any of its activities until the marketing department has acquired customer orders or informs production control that an estimated date of completion should be prepared for a bid which marketing can submit. It must also wait for the engineering department to complete the product and process analysis and supply personnel and machine operation time data.

Production management will use the schedules and charts showing the allocation of machine capacity as the basis for decisions regarding overtime, or expansion or reduction of work hours or of the work-force. If the projected schedules indicate the need for more materials or machinery, the purchasing department can receive this information in advance of the need. In this way, it will not be hurried in its purchasing activities, which might result in higher costs or less desirable materials or machines. The personnel department, with advance notice of manpower needs, can acquire the best possible workers. This would not be possible if it were told to hire additional workers immediately. The maintenance department can be notified as to what machines and equipment will be necessary for next week's production and can give these first priority.

Although production control is a staff department whose function is primarily to assist the line departments, it exercises considerable functional authority. While this does not entail issuing orders to any line personnel, it does give this department the responsibility and authority for routing procedures and for scheduling the work to the various departments. Line staff conflict does not often develop even though functional authority is exercised by the production control department. This is because foremen recognize that the activities of this staff department are helpful to them and can save them time which can be used profitably elsewhere.

PRODUCTION CONTROL SYSTEMS

The two major classifications of production control systems are related to the two major types of production activity, that is, continuous production and intermittent production. The control system for the former is usually called *flow control* while the control of the latter is referred to as *order* or *batch control*.

When production is continuous the primary purpose of the production control system is to control the rate at which the product flows through the facility. Since a continuous production system manufactures standard products produced for inventory, the machinery required, the work assignments and the sequence of operations are all fixed. Consequently, scheduling problems and considerations are taken into account at the time the layout of the facility is established. Also, since the process is fixed and repetitive, there is no need to generate route sheets and operational instructions with each item produced. However, in such an operation the availability of parts and materials when needed is extremely important. The shortage of a single required part can shut down production entirely.

When production is intermittent we have what is generally called a *job shop*. A job shop handles a variety of orders from different customers. Each order usually requires special processing. A job shop is much more difficult to control than a continuous production operation because each order tends to be unique, that is, different in some respect from every other order.

In a job shop, similar machines or similar functional activities are grouped into work centers. When the number of orders being processed is large, scheduling becomes a serious problem. Job shops are not restricted to manufacturing organizations but are common in various types of service businesses also. Restaurants and health care facilities typify job shop operations in the service area.

In order control, the principal concern is processing each order through the facility. Route sheets and operation sheets provide the processing instructions. Production control is responsible for insuring availability of all the productive factors required. These include labor, material and machinery. When all factors have been verified, production control releases work orders which authorize production to start. Once a job is released by a work order, progress reports are required periodically to indicate the status of each job until it is completed.

The diversity of production systems is so great that attempting to cover them in any great detail here would simply be confusing. However, since most systems involve to some degree the four phases of routing, scheduling, dispatching, and follow-up, it should be helpful to discuss these activities to the extent necessary to clarify what they entail.

Routing

The first step in routing is to break the product down into its component parts and then determine the materials needed to make the parts. This problem frequently is simplified when the customer provides the blueprints and the lists of parts and materials to be used. When these are not provided, the production control department must acquire them. Engineers and technicians capable of providing the necessary data may be assigned to this task. In most cases, the engineering department will be asked to provide this information for production control. The bill of materials is a detailed list of parts and components needed for the product's manufacture. Any questions concerning the quality specifications of materials and production tolerances must be resolved at this time.

The bill of materials should indicate the quantity needed for production. Provision should also be made for the production of replacement parts and for spoilage.

Other aspects of the routing function include the determination of the proper sequence of assembly operations as well as the fabrication of materials. For each material used in the product, every step in its processing should be detailed and the best operational sequence determined. The time required for each operation and each machine and the machine capacity must also be known or estimated. The time for machine operations can be estimated by using times for comparable elements from past records. This assumes that the conditions surrounding the present manufacturing orders, such as labor skill needed, condition of machines and equipment, type of material and quantity to be produced are similar to those that existed earlier. In addition to listing the machines that can be used in each of the operations, the following standards are included for each machine: setup time, time to complete the designated operation, and the number of pieces that can be completed per unit of time.

Production control continues its routing after it has accumulated all of this process information. Its duty is to plan which machine should be used for each operation, so that machines can be utilized fully with the lowest unit costs and fastest production time. Quite often, full machine utilization, low cost, and rapid production cannot be met, and one factor may have to be compromised to accomplish the others. For example, a higher-cost procedure may be necessary in order to meet a scheduled delivery date if the low-cost machine is not available for reasons of prior commitments or maintenance problems.

The machine with the greatest capacity may not be the cheapest to use. Although its operating costs may be low, it may require a long setup time. For a small order, it is more economical to use a slower machine that has a low setup cost, even if its operating cost is high. The combination of both costs may result in a lower per unit cost in the latter case.

To gain maximum machine utilization, production control should have knowledge of the flexibility of the machines. By routing operations to the machines of limited capabilities first, the more flexible machines can be used for other purposes. If this procedure were reversed, the former machines might not be utilized and delays in production could result.

The route sheet is the summary of all the routing activity. All of the manufacturing data are recorded on the route sheet. This includes all materials with the part number and description; the quantity of each material; a complete list of operations required and in the proper sequence; the type of machine and equipment for each operation; the standard setup time and per piece time with each machine; the department where the machine is located; and the labor grade which should be used for the operation. The route sheet also will specify where inspections will be made during the manufacturing process. The route sheet is sometimes called an operations sheet, operations ticket, shop travel card, instruction sheet, or specification sheet.

The route sheet should serve as the foundation for all other production control department activities. In order to reduce the cost and confusion of paperwork, the route sheet may be the only record used for manufacturing operations by the production control department. When this is the case, the route sheet serves as a progress report; it will have additional columns for recording the scheduled beginning and completion dates, times for each operation and the actual starting and finishing dates.

Once engineering has prepared the basic data concerning a product for the production control department, the information is filed. As future orders are received for the same product, the route sheets can be prepared in a minimum of time. This does not mean that engineering should be bypassed when repeat orders are received. Significant changes may have occurred since the original product and process analyses were made, which may change the material requirements or the processes or their sequence.

Standard procedure should require approval by engineering of all materials lists and sequence-of-operations lists for each customer order before the route sheet is prepared.

Scheduling

When beginning and completion times and dates are set for each step of the manufacturing process, they provide fixed points as bases for reference. These enable the establishment of goals that should be attained by the company line and staff departments. The provision of the time element for the various stages permits the coordination of the necessary facilities.

In order to establish schedules it is necessary to determine the time necessary for accomplishing the required work. In manufacturing this involves the production of the component parts, the subassemblies and the final assembly of the finished product. Much of the required information can be obtained from the route sheet. The route sheet however does not show nonproductive or idle time and this must also be considered in establishing schedules.

At least two schedules are involved in production control activities. These are the *master schedule* and the *production schedule*. The master schedule is the first schedule developed. The master schedule is based on machine and plant capacity and balances overall production requirements against these constraints. This enables the production control department to see whether customer delivery dates given by the marketing department can be met. If there is any doubt that the dates can be met, this difficulty can be discussed immediately between marketing and the customer. When the problem occurs at this point, many customers may agree to accept a later delivery. If this is not possible, production control can give the order special attention so that it can be scheduled to meet the original delivery date. Marketing may be able to arrange for a later date for a different order. The master schedule permits a closer coordination between marketing and manufacturing, and production control can keep marketing advised of the earliest delivery commitment dates based upon orders already scheduled and available plant capacity.

The master schedule is a periodic (weekly, monthly or quarterly) record of the hours available for each type of machine or each department. As new orders come into the plant, the time required to fill them from each type of machine or from each department is deducted from hours previously available.

The master schedule can also be used as a basis for top management decisions such as the possible need for overtime operations, the need for a second shift, additional machinery or even plant expansion. In a cyclical or seasonal downturn, the master schedule may show a large amount of idle capacity. When this occurs, management must decide how to meet this problem: take on new products, do subcontracting work, go on short hours or lay off part of its workforce. In any case, the master schedule brings the situation to the attention of management.

The production schedule is a detailed analysis of all the operations in manufacturing a customer order. All of the delivery dates that have been accepted on the master schedule can be further verified. The preparation of the production schedule necessitates working backward from the delivery date to determine the relative relationships between the starting and ending dates for each assembly and fabrication. The time data necessary for preparing this schedule are found on the route sheet.

Production scheduling is concerned with the allocation of productive capacity to every operation in the process. This includes personnel assignments as well as machine loading. Machine loading assigns work to machines so that fabrication takes place during specified time periods. This allocation of machine and labor capacity tends to assure a continuous flow of work and reduces idle time.

In diversified production, a customer orders a specified quantity which determines the amount produced. Where different orders are received for identical products, it may be possible to manufacture them in one lot. By so doing, the machine setup costs are incurred only once and the costs can be spread over a larger volume of production. In some cases, different products may require the same parts. By combining the operations necessary in the fabrication of the part, some savings may be gained. With an efficient scheduling operation, these procedures lead to lower costs and added profits.

The production schedule should be flexible enough to accommodate emergencies that may occur. These might include machine breakdowns or special customer rush orders. Emergencies can be met by not scheduling productive capacity to the limit.

Dispatching

The dispatching function authorizes the actual manufacturing activities. That is, it authorizes the issuance of necessary materials, the use of machines and the assignment of labor. It also expedites the production activities. Dispatching sees that the right materials are in the right place at the proper time with the required facilities and personnel to do the job.

Dispatching is essentially a clerical function performed by members of the production control department who are located in each of the manufacturing departments. They are there to help expedite the work and to assist the foreman. Dispatchers help find misplaced materials and tools, and errors in manufacturing, make minor adjustments in schedules to compensate for delays, and suggest corrective measures which may improve operations.

Records of idle machine time and the reasons for their occurrence are kept by the dispatcher. Any difference between scheduled and completed quantities is recorded and sent to the production control department also. The paperwork in production control is simplified by the use of route sheets for all of the actual manufacturing operations. The dispatchers in each department receive multiple copies of each route sheet. These serve as manufacturing orders which authorize work to be done.

One copy of the route sheet is used as a requisition for materials. Another copy is used as a time ticket for the worker who is to do each operation when he receives the materials. The dates and starting and ending time for each job are recorded and the worker carries out the instructions for his operation. The route sheet shows the labor grade and rate, and since it contains other information such as the quantity produced and the elapsed work time, it is the basis for labor cost computation.

Materials handlers receive their instructions directly from the dispatchers or the route sheet which tells them where the next operation is located so that materials and assemblies can be moved with a minimum of delay. Prompt movement of the work between operations and departments can reduce the nonproductive time.

As each stage of the manufacturing cycle is completed, the dispatcher receives the route sheets with the dates, starting and finishing times recorded. This information is relayed to the production control department which records the information on the master route sheet. When the order is completed, all copies of the route sheet should be returned to the central production control office.

Follow-up

Follow-up is the control function of production planning and control. It is concerned with the progress record of the actual manufacturing activity in the plant as compared with the scheduled volume of output. The follow-up procedure uncovers any deviations between these figures and brings them to the attention of the line organization. The extent and duration of the discrepancy is the basis for determining which management level will be given the responsibility for finding a solution.

That part of the dispatcher's duties which involves production expediting can be considered an integral part of the follow-up function. The minor revisions that the dispatcher may make in the machine-load charts also are part of follow-up or control. These adjustments, plus others such as the use of standby equipment and short periods of overtime put into effect by the foreman, are ways in which attempts are made to bring the actual dates and times of starting and completion in line with the scheduled figures.

Problems may arise that will cause a greater divergency in quantity and duration between the actual and scheduled figures. This situation may result from excessive machine breakdown or absenteeism. These factors are beyond the control of the foreman, thus the production control records would have to go to a higher line manager who would attempt to solve the problems.

Each level of management will handle problems in line with the responsibility and authority delegated to it. Thus the plant manager may have the foreman make all decisions when production is one day or less behind schedule; up to three days behind schedule may fall within the province of the department head; and beyond this, the plant manager. This is an application of organizational principle number 4 discussed at the end of Chapter 3.

Production control should also concern itself with production that is ahead of schedule. While this can be considered as normal occasionally, the situation should be subjected to evaluation if it occurs too often. It may mean that scheduling standards are not appropriate or that the plant efficiency is higher than originally estimated. Possibly a new procedure has been incorporated which has significantly reduced the time for doing the work, and the standards have not been changed.

To some extent the activities described above are present in all types of production systems. However, production systems vary to such a great extent that no single production control procedure or set of procedures will be applicable to every type of operation. Nevertheless, efficient production planning and control are necessary in any profit maximization program. A great deal of profit is lost or eroded through idle machine time, idle personnel time, production bottlenecks, etc. that could have been reduced or even eliminated by the institution of effective production planning and control.

Let's now take a look at production control as it applies to a job shop, that is, where the production is intermittent and the product is manufactured to order.

ORDER PRODUCTION CONTROL

Although certainly not a fixed rule, mass production appears most common in large-scale operations. The most common production system for a small business appears to be the job shop. There are certainly many exceptions, and of course when discussing medium-sized businesses, it becomes difficult to generalize. However, since order control in job shop or semi-job shop operations represents the more difficult aspects of production control, special attention will be devoted to these problems.

The primary objective in order control is to process each order most efficiently through the facility. The four stage process of routing, scheduling, dispatching, and follow-up all apply in job shop operations, but the major problems usually occur in scheduling. Scheduling in the job shop involves four steps:

1. Allocation of jobs to work centers,
2. Establishing a system of job priorities at each work center,
3. Revising priorities as new jobs are received and conditions change,
4. Monitoring job progress.

The allocation of jobs to work centers is called *loading* or *shop loading*. Although loading assigns jobs to work centers, it does not necessarily specify the sequence in which the jobs are to be performed at the center. The problem of loading becomes more complex as more alternative work centers become available for a particular job. If there are no choices to be made—that is, only one work center is available—then the loading problem is very simple. When two or more work centers are available and able to perform the same job, then the loading problem can become complex. The choice among work centers can be based upon costs, the skills and efficiency of the personnel, or upon other jobs which must also be assigned. Various methods can be used for loading, ranging from simple management judgment or intuition to complicated mathematical methods. Although judgment and intuition are fine in simple loading situations, they generally cannot provide optimal assignments particularly when the situation is complex. In order to avoid delays, bottlenecks, missed delivery dates and other problems which result in profit erosion, several objective methods are available to provide optimal solutions. One relatively simple yet effective method belongs to the general procedure called *linear programming*. This technique is called the *assignment method* of linear programming.

The Assignment Method for Loading

The assignment method is a simple method for assigning n jobs to n work centers on the basis of some measure of value such as cost to process or time to process. The optimal assignment will minimize time or cost as the case may be. To begin, a matrix must be established for jobs vs. work centers. In order to use the assignment method, the number of jobs and the number of work centers should be equal, resulting in a square matrix. When this requirement cannot be met, then dummy rows or columns must be added to make the matrix square. When the assignment method is used, jobs cannot be split among work centers. If any of the possible assignments are not feasible, that assignment is given a very large value that will prohibit its occurrence.

The general procedure is to attempt to generate zeros in some of the cells of the matrix. Since we are attempting to minimize some measure of performance, cost or time, assignments involving only zero-valued cells would be optimal. Zeros are generated by subtracting the lowest value in each column from every other value in that column and the lowest value in each row from every other value in that row. The procedure can best be illustrated with an example.

Consider the case of Acme Precision Manufacturing Company, a job shop that produces parts to customer specifications. Five jobs from customers A, B, C, D, and E must be assigned to machines. Five machines are available and each of the machines (and machinists) can do any of the five jobs. The time required for each job at each of the five machines is provided below. The optimal assignment will minimize the time required for all five jobs.

Machine

JOB	#1	#2	#3	#4	#5
A	3	8	10	6	3
B	5	4	6	9	5
C	4	3	8	7	6
D	8	5	9	8	4
E	2	7	8	5	8

Step 1. Subtract the lowest value in each column from every other value in the same column with the following results:

Machine

JOB	#1	#2	#3	#4	#5
A	1	5	4	1	0
B	3	1	0	4	2
C	2	0	2	2	3
D	6	2	3	3	1
E	0	4	2	0	5

Step 2. Subtract the lowest value in each row from every other value in the same row. Then draw the minimum number of lines that can cover all of the zeros as shown below:

Machine

JOB	#1	#2	#3	#4	#5
A	1	5	4	1	0
B	3	1	0	4	2
C	2	0	2	2	3
D	5	1	2	2	0
E	0	4	2	0	5

If the minimum number of lines equals the number of rows and columns, then an optimal assignment has been reached. If the minimum number of lines is less than the number of rows and columns, further modification of the matrix is necessary. In this case it required only four lines to cover all the zeros, therefore, another step is necessary.

Step 3. Subtract the smallest cell entry *not* covered by a line from every other *uncovered* cell entry. Then add the value of that entry to all cell entries that are intersected by two lines. The smallest uncovered cell entry is 1. The new matrix is:

Machine

JOB	#1	#2	#3	#4	#5
A	0	5	4	0	0
B	2	1	0	3	2
C	1	0	2	1	2
D	4	1	2	1	0
E	0	5	3	0	6

All of the zeros can now be covered by five lines which is equal to the number of rows and the number of columns, therefore, an optimal assignment can now be made. This is done by first finding columns and rows which contain a single zero. Columns 2 and 3 each have a single zero as do rows B, C, and D. The assignments are made as follows:

Job B to Machine 3
Job C to Machine 2
Job D to Machine 5

The remaining jobs can be assigned to any work center having a zero in the cell. That is, A could go to either #1, #4, or #5. However, since job D was already assigned to machine #5, A is limited to either #1 or #4. Job E can also be assigned to either machine #1 or machine #4. Either assignment would be optimal. It is obvious from this example that there may be more than one optimal assignment. The two optimal assignments in this case would be:

OPTIMAL ASSIGNMENT 1	OPTIMAL ASSIGNMENT 2
A to 1	A to 4
B to 3	B to 3
C to 2	C to 2
D to 5	D to 5
E to 4	E to 1

The time required under both optimal assignments is:

OPTIMAL ASSIGNMENT 1	TIME REQUIRED	OPTIMAL ASSIGNMENT 2	TIME REQUIRED
A to 1	3	A to 4	6
B to 3	6	B to 3	6
C to 2	3	C to 2	3
D to 5	4	D to 5	4
E to 4	5	E to 1	2
Total	21	Total	21

The minimum time required for all five jobs is 21 hours.

The Index Method for Loading

A quick and simple method for shop loading, called the *index method,* is an alternative to the assignment method previously discussed. The index method, like the assignment method, does not allow for job splitting; however, it does not require a square matrix of jobs versus work centers. The index method does not always provide an optimal assignment, however, it usually results in reasonably good ones.

   Given a matrix of jobs versus work centers in terms of time to perform or cost to perform, an index is developed for each job at each work center. The index is determined by dividing the lowest value (time or cost) for the job into the value at all of the possible work centers. The lowest index number for a job will therefore be 1.00. Jobs are always assigned first to a work center having an index for that job of 1.00 so long as the capacity for that work center is not exceeded. Then assignmnets are made in order of increasing index value.

   We will illustrate the index method with the same data used for the assignment method. The data refer to the Precision Manufacturing Company problem. The matrix of jobs versus machines will be the same with the values in the cells representing hours. The additional information added here will be hours available for that day on each machine. Although this problem involves five jobs and five machines, a square matrix, this is not a necessary requirement for the index method.

| | Machine | | | | |
JOB	#1	#2	#3	#4	#5
A	3	8	10	6	3
B	5	4	6	9	5
C	4	3	8	7	9
D	8	5	9	8	4
E	2	7	8	5	8
Capacity	4	6	8	8	4

   The first step is to assign the index to each job at each machine by dividing the smallest value in each row into every other value in that row. This results in the following matrix:

Machine

JOB	#1		#2		#3		#4		#5	
	HRS.	INDEX	HRS.	INDEX	HRS.	INDEX	HRS.	INDEX	HRS.	INDEX
A	3	1.00	8	2.67	10	3.33	6	2.00	3	1.00
B	5	1.25	4	1.00	6	1.50	9	2.25	5	1.25
C	4	1.33	3	1.00	8	2.67	7	2.33	6	2.00
D	8	2.00	5	1.25	9	2.25	8	2.00	4	1.00
E	2	1.00	7	3.50	8	4.00	5	2.50	8	4.00

The assignments are then made as follows

Machine

JOB	#1		#2		#3		#4		#5	
	HRS.	INDEX	HRS.	INDEX	HRS.	INDEX	HRS.	INDEX	HRS.	INDEX
A	3	1.00								
B			4	1.00						
C							7	2.33		
D									4	1.00
E					8	4.00				
Assigned	3		4		8		7		4	
Capacity	4		6		8		8		4	

Starting with job A, it could have been assigned either to #1 or #5 since the index at both machines was 1.00. Assigning job A to #1, we use up 3 of the 4 hours available on that machine. Job B is assigned to #2, having an index of 1.00 on that machine and using 4 of the 6 hours available. Job C has an index of 1.00 on machine #2, but the hours required would exceed that machine's capacity. The next lowest indexes for C are on machines #1 and #5 but in both cases the capacities of those machines would be exceeded. Consequently, job C is assigned to machine #4 with an index of 2.33. This procedure is followed until all jobs are assigned.

PRODUCTION CONTROL IN SERVICE OPERATIONS

Service operations have problems similar to those of manufacturing systems in controlling operations. There are however two primary differences that create special problems. These differences result from the inability to stockpile (or inventory) services and the extreme variability of demand.

In manufacturing operations, particularly continuous production processes, inventories smooth out fluctuations in demand. When demand declines, goods can be stored in inventory which is drawn upon when demand increases. By adding to and drawing from inventory, production schedules can be maintained at a constant level, and problems of material and labor shortages or surpluses can generally be avoided. Services however cannot be inventoried. Services must be available when demanded, and during periods of low or no demand, the service providers are idle. Since most service operations are labor intensive, this means that fluctuations in the requirement for labor will match fluctuations in the demand for the service.

To some degree the assignment or scheduling problem in a service operation is similar to that in a job shop operation. In a job shop, work is performed to order, not for stocking inventory. Demand can be variable, resulting in a surplus of jobs to be performed in one time period and a shortage of jobs in another. In a job shop, jobs are received, and jobs are scheduled. In a service facility it is more usual to think in terms of scheduling personnel and facilities rather than jobs. But assigning jobs to facilities or facilities to jobs are simply two different ways of looking at the same process.

Although the process of scheduling jobs and that of scheduling facilities may be the same essential process, often the criteria may differ. In scheduling jobs, the principle considerations are meeting required job completion dates, maximizing output and utilizing the facilities most efficiently. In scheduling facilities or resources, particularly when the principal resource is personnel, other considerations may take precedence. These would include the wishes and desires of personnel for specific schedules or certain shifts, vacation and holiday schedules, and so on.

Tech-Ed Schools, Inc.

As described previously, Tech-Ed Schools, Inc. is a proprietary business and technical school. However, the production control (that is, scheduling problem experienced by Tech-Ed) is similar to that of other schools and colleges, hospitals, and service operations. To some extent the school problem may be simpler than that of other service operations, such as hospitals, where demand can become quite erratic. Since Tech-Ed operates on a trimester basis (that is, three sessions of equal length each year), scheduling is on a trimester basis rather than on a daily or weekly basis as in some other kinds of service operations.

The primary scheduling problem for Tech-Ed involves the scheduling of classes and the assignment of students, faculty and facilities to those classes. The most important input into the scheduling process is a forecast of student enrollments in general and the demand for the courses offered in particular. The physical constraints on the process include the classroom space and the number of available faculty qualified to teach the courses offered. Other considerations must include the desires of the faculty in terms of schedules, number of class preparations and so on.

Tech-Ed forecasts for three trimesters at a time, that is, for one year. Schedules are based on the number and distribution of students among the various courses offered. Tech-Ed uses part-time instructors when demand exceeds the forecast demand. Occasionally, classes must be taught with few students attending when demand turns out to be much less than forecast. In order to avoid overestimating demand, Tech-Ed's forecasts are usually conservative. It is better to underestimate demand and use part-time instructors when necessary than to overestimate demand and be forced to utilize staff inefficiently. This criteria may not however apply to a hospital, for example.

In general, in scheduling services it is necessary to try to match resources to demand. Since demand cannot be controlled and inventorying services is impossible, the use of part-time labor, overtime, and other incentives such as off-peak or nonprime time rates to encourage a leveling of demand are tools that must be used. Scheduling techniques for facilities or resources are similar to those used for scheduling jobs. These include the assignment method of linear programming and the index method, both illustrated in the previous section.

ALLOCATION OF RESOURCES

A problem facing entrepreneurs and managers that is related to production planning and control is that of allocating resources. The resources available at any point in time are always limited and often scarce. These include capital, labor, materials, machinery, etc. At the same time there are usually conflicting demands for these resources. Management always works to allocate these resources in such a way as to optimize some measure of business performance, usually profits. However, determining the optimal allocation is not easy and some objective method for doing so can help in maximizing profits. Such a method is linear programming. We have already illustrated the assignment method of linear programming for job shop loading, however, the applications of this useful technique are far broader than that. One major application is to determine the optimal allocation of limited resources to jobs or projects.

In order for a problem to be amenable to solution using linear programming it must meet certain requirements. First, the organization must have an objective it wants to achieve. This objective in terms of a profit maximization program would be to maximize profits or some other factor related to profits such as contribution. This objective must be expressed in the form of a linear equation. In fact, the equation which expresses the objective to be achieved is called the *objective function.*

Second, there must be alternatives available, one of which will achieve the objective. These various alternatives require the commitment of limited resources. The limitations on the resources are called *constraints* and the constraints must be expressed as a set of linear *inequalities.* Inequalities use the signs ≤ (less than or equal to) or ≥ (greater than or equal to) to relate the variables in the constraints whereas an equation uses the = sign for that purpose. Consequently, an equation is a great deal more restrictive than an inequality.

Consider a simple problem using Westwinds, Inc. as an example. Referring to their forecast and production plans for a coming period, management finds that excess capacity exists in manufacturing. If this excess capacity can be used to produce additional revenue, the profit for that period could be increased. The market forecasts indicate that simply expanding production of one of their standard products would not be profitable, consequently the excess capacity should be put to some other use.

Two products which had not previously been put in production due to their limited markets are a large ventilating fan, the VC20, and a small 5000 Btu room air conditioner, the Mark 5. If these can be used to take up the available capacity, profits could be increased. Each VC20 contributes $20.00 to profit while each Mark 5 sold contributes $35.

The limited resource which must be allocated in this case is *capacity,* that is, the time available in the manufacturing departments which are required to produce the products. The departments involved are fabrication and assembly.

Each VC20 requires three hours in fabrication and two hours in assembly. Each Mark 5 requires two hours in fabrication and four hours in assembly. The total capacity available is 120 hours in fabrication and 160 hours in assembly. The problem is to determine the best possible combination of products to produce and sell in order to realize the maximum profit. These data can be summarized as follows.

HOURS REQUIRED PER UNIT

	VC 20	MARK 10	TOTAL HOURS AVAILABLE
Fabrication	3	2	120
Assembly	2	4	160
Profit per unit	$20	$35	

In order to solve the allocation problem the information must be stated in the form of mathematical equations or inequalities. The objective function will be in the form of an equation. Abbreviating VC20 with the letter V and Mark 10 with the letter M, we can state that profit is equal to $20 times V plus $35 times M. That is, the objective function which we seek to maximize is:

$$P = 20\,V + 35\,M$$

The time used in manufacturing some combination of these two products must not exceed the total time available in the fabrication and assembly departments. That is, the time required to make V times the number of V's produced plus the time required to make M times the number of M's produced must be less than or equal to the time available in each department. Expressing these constraints in the form of linear inequalities, we get for each department:

Fabrication: $3V + 2M \leq 120$
Assembly: $2V + 4M \leq 160$

We will find the optimal allocation using the graphic method.

Step 1. Set up a graph with the horizontal scale representing the number of Mark 10s produced and vertical scale representing the number of VC20s.

Step 2. Plot the constraints on the graph as equalities, that is plot

$$3V + 2M = 120$$

and

$$2V + 4M = 160$$

Since the 120 and 160 are the limits on the constraints, any point enclosed by both lines will satisfy the constraints, that is, would represent a feasible but not necessarily optimal solution. The shaded area in Figure 9.1 represents the feasible solution.

The optimal solution occurs at the point where the two lines intersect. By drawing the graph accurately, we can determine that the optimal solution is to produce 20 VC20s and 30 Mark 10s.

Substituting these values back into the objective function, we can find that the optimal contribution to profit would be:

$$
\begin{aligned}
P &= 20V + 35M \\
&= 20\,(20) + 35\,(30) \\
&= 400 + 1050 \\
&= 1450
\end{aligned}
$$

No other combination of these two products that satisfies the constraints can produce a higher contribution to profit.

If there are more than two constraints, there will be more than a single intersection of the lines on the graph. The optimal solution will occur at one of the intersections or corners. Each corner point can be

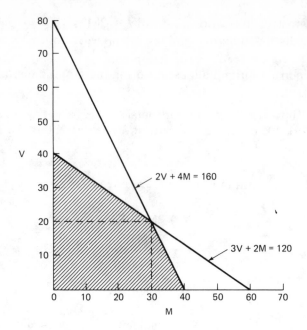

Figure 9.1. Graphical solution to Westwind resource allocation problem

tested by substitution into the objective function and the point providing the largest value of contribution to profit is optimal.

The graphic solution is effective so long as the number of variables in the problem (products, jobs, etc.) is no greater than three. When the number of variables exceeds three, other analytical methods are available. For solving resource allocation problems in small and medium-sized businesses, the graphic method is frequently sufficient. When more complex methods are required, computer programs are available to provide the manager with the solutions. Therefore, these methods will not be illustrated here.

SUMMARY

Production control is a broad term encompassing a variety of activities necessary to operate a production system most efficiently. Poor production planning and control can cause profit erosion through production bottlenecks, delays, inefficient use of facilities, idle and wasted time, and so on. In addition to the specific activities and tools discussed here, including methods of job loading, resource allocation, etc., effective production control is also dependent upon accurate capacity planning, efficient purchasing and effective inventory control. A breakdown in any of these areas can have significant effects in the production area resulting in profit erosion.

10. Establishing and Controlling Quality Standards

Probably the most important commodity that any enterprise has to offer its customers is the quality of its product or service. A reputation for meeting its commitments, for delivering what it promises or contracts to deliver, or in general for delivering a product or service that performs the function it was intended to perform in the way that the user has the right to anticipate, is one of the most valuable assets that a business organization can possess. Conversely, failure to deliver or to meet the performance anticipation that the customer has a right to expect can be one of the surest guarantees of business failure.

What has all this to do with quality? It is quite obvious that the ability to deliver is a function of planning, inventories, scheduling, production control and the other business functions already discussed. It is not so obvious that these and many other functions all contribute to the overall quality of the product or service supplied. Establishing, maintaining, and controlling standards of quality is the subject of this chapter. Without such standards and the procedures for maintaining them all the other functions could be an exercise in futility. In terms of profit maximization, poor quality leads to profit erosion in the short run and the probability of bankruptcy over the longer term.

Despite the importance of quality and its control or assurance, it is surprising how little is generally known and understood about this concept as it applies to business and industrial organizations. Traditionally quality control has been associated with manufacturing industry and the manufactured product. Even though the majority of quality control applications are still found in manufacturing operations, recently the quality control concept and its associated techniques have also been directed toward control or assurance of quality in many nonmanufacturing processes. It is important to emphasize however that all processes to which quality control techniques can be applied are involved in the production of something, whether it is a product, a piece of paper, information or a service. In fact, the principal and only requirement for applying quality control is simply the existence of a production process for a good or service for which some standard of quality can be specified and whose output can be measured in quantitative terms.

WHAT CONSTITUTES QUALITY

The word quality has different meanings depending upon the context in which it is being used and on who is using it. In the context of quality control, quality is simply some characteristic of a product or process for which a standard can be established. This may not be a very precise definition, but then quality is not a very precise concept.

The characteristic that constitutes quality will differ depending upon the nature of the product or process with which it is associated. For example, quality characteristics of a television receiver might be the clarity of the picture, the sensitivity to weak signals and its reliability. Quality characteristics of a restaurant would probably include the swiftness or attentiveness of the service, the variety of the offerings on the menu, and the tastiness of the food served. The quality of a commuter train service might be measured by the promptness of the service and the condition of the railroad cars.

It is apparent that quality applies not only to products, but also to services or operations. Furthermore, a wide variety of characteristics can be used to describe the quality of even a single item. That is, a single product or process can have several characteristics descriptive of its quality. For these reasons, it is extremely important in the context of quality control to specify quite clearly and unambiguously those specific attributes of the product or process that constitute the quality to be controlled.

When considering the control of some quality characteristic, it is necessary to specify exactly what level of the characteristic constitutes good or acceptable quality and what constitutes poor or unacceptable quality. In ordinary conversation, good quality and poor quality are loosely used terms. In quality control, more precision is required. However, quality in the context of quality control does not necessarily mean best in some absolute sense. It is instead a matter of degree.

Good quality simply implies that the product or service to which the term is applied conforms to the standards or requirements established for it. In other words, the product or service performs or is performed in the intended manner. This is an important point and warrants some additional comment.

It is often assumed that good quality refers to some absolute standard. This is simply not true. In that sense, the quality of a fast food restaurant could never approach that of an expensive gourmet restaurant. And, in the absolute sense, that is probably true. However, this is not the meaning of quality in the context of quality control. Different quality standards apply to the two different types of restaurants. Excellence of the food served without regard to price and the attentiveness of the service might be the important quality characteristics of the gourmet restaurant. Plain, well-prepared, moderately priced food and efficiency of service might constitute the quality characteristics of the fast food restaurant. While a dinner for two might cost close to $100.00 at the former and extend over three hours, a dinner for two at the latter would probably cost one-tenth of that amount and be completed in a half hour or less. Obviously the quality standards to be applied to both establishments should be quite different. In terms of quality control, the quality of both might be excellent depending upon how closely each adheres to its established standards. It is interesting to note that the market to a great extent determines the applicable quality standards.

Quality then is simply some measurable characteristic of a product, process or service. In order to be controlled it must be measurable. That is, various levels of the quality characteristic must be observable in terms of numerical values or must be capable of being converted to numerical values. Any operation for which a quality characteristic can be specified and then observed or measured in numerical terms is subject to quality control.

The advantages of establishing standards of quality and maintaining those standards should be apparent to any business embarking on a profit maximization program. Poor quality results in excessive costs and profit erosion. The costs are due to waste, duplication of effort and the loss of customer goodwill. To the extent that these costs can be reduced or eliminated, the profit picture of the organization will benefit.

STANDARDS

The standards established for any product or operation are dependent upon whether we are referring to a manufactured product or to a service. Standards may be tight or they may be loose. There are however only two criteria that must be observed. First, the standards must be reasonable. Establishing standards that are impossible to meet, rather than improving quality, could have exactly the opposite effect. Impossible standards lead to frustration and negative results. In the discipline of quality control this is referred to as standards which exceed the capability of the process. Second, the standards must be expressed in quantitative terms, and performance vis à vis the standards must be measurable. Otherwise it would be impossible to determine whether the standards are being met and also to measure the amount of deviation from the standards if they are not. The quality control process involves these three basic steps:

1. Establishment of standards
2. Comparison of performance with the standards
3. Corrective action whenever performance deviates from the standards

Appropriate standards may vary from a production standard that specifies that a particular part must have a diameter of 5.5 cm ± 0.01 cm to a standard that states that a customer approaching a teller's window at any branch of the Northeastern National Bank should not have to wait in line longer than 3.5 minutes before being served. Both of these standards are expressed in numerical terms. Observations of actual performance are measurable in the same terms and it is possible to compare these observations with the standards to determine whether or not the standards are being met in practice. It is also possible from the observations to determine the amount of deviation from the standard that occurs if they are not being met and what steps should be taken to bring the actual performance up to the standard.

Though we already mentioned that a standard must not exceed the capability of the process to which it is applied, we didn't pursue this interesting concept of process capability. In the previous examples we simply assumed that the established standards were consistent with the capability of the processes described, but this was not apparent from the information presented. In some instances the capability of the process is determined by the physical properties of the process itself. If, in the first case, the technical capabilities of the machines and personnel turning out the part for which the standard was established are incapable of the precision specified (that is, a tolerance of ± 0.01 cm), then no management decision can make the standard attainable. If management has committed itself to a contract with that provision without determining if the process has the capability to meet the provision, then a large number of defective parts will be produced which will have to be removed before delivery can be made to the customer.

In the second case, if the standard is not being met, it is possible that the process can be improved if management is willing to commit additional resources for that purpose. This might be done by having enough additional tellers on hand to accommodate the maximum demand anticipated so that whenever a waiting line exceeds some specified length, another window could be opened. Of course, the application of additional resources in order to meet stringent standards entails additional cost. A consideration of the various quality costs and how they interact is worth any manager's attention.

QUALITY COSTS

When considering the cost of quality, the manager should think in terms of those costs the organization incurs attempting to achieve and maintain some specified level of product quality and also in terms of those costs it incurs by failing to do so. In other words, costs are associated with the achievement and maintenance of good quality, and costs can be associated with failures in this respect, that is, with poor quality. So long as the costs of poor quality are greater than the costs of maintaining good quality, it is prudent to expend resources on quality improvement. When a given quality improvement costs more to achieve than the savings that would result, then the additional expenditure is not warranted. In a sense, this is an application of the break-even analysis principle discussed in a previous chapter. The point at which cost savings equal the cost of achieving those savings represents an optimal level of expenditure. In order to find that optimal point, it is necessary to identify and examine the different kinds of quality costs involved.

The costs of establishing and maintaining good quality can be divided into two categories: *appraisal costs* and *prevention costs*. Prevention costs are those costs incurred to prevent defective product or defective operations or processes from occurring in the first place. Included in this category are quality control engineering costs and employee quality training. The former applies primarily to manufacturing operations, but the latter is important in all types of business organizations. Appraisal costs include the expenses incurred in appraising and evaluating the level of quality achieved by the organization either at some point in time or on a continuing basis. In manufacturing these costs include inspection, capability studies, product testing and other similar activities. In general, any evaluation of operations, processes or products designed to determine if established quality standards are being met falls into this category.

The costs of poor quality are generally called *failure costs*. Failure costs result from defective materials and from products that fail to meet the specifications established for them. They also result from personnel carelessness, failure to follow approved procedures, lack of adequate training and so on. The actual costs that result are *rework costs*, that is, the cost of doing something over, the cost of scrap and wasted material, wasted time, spoilage, and customer ill will.

Failure costs can be divided into internal failure costs and external failure costs. Any cost due to a failure of the system, product or material in the plant (that is, within the organization) comes under the category of internal failure costs. These are generally the costs of scrap, waste, rework, etc. Costs incurred due to failure outside of the plant are external failure costs. These include product service attributable to correcting defects in the product, servicing of complaints and of course the intangible costs of customer ill will.

In terms of the total quality costs, it has been estimated that in most companies about 70% of quality costs are failure costs while 25% and 5% are appraisal and prevention costs. These figures would seem to indicate a considerable imbalance between the various kinds of quality costs. Since those expenditures in the prevention and appraisal areas are made for the purpose of reducing failure costs, it would seem that there is still a great deal of room in most companies for expenditures on appraisal of quality and the prevention of defects or failures. A chart depicting the relationship and behavior of these costs for various levels of quality is provided in Figure 10.1.

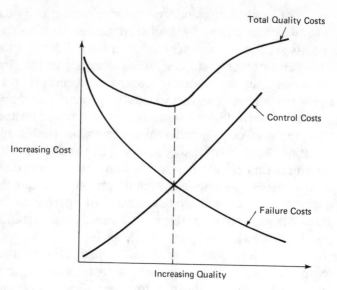

Figure 10.1. Quality cost relationships.

The costs of appraisal and prevention are considered controllable costs. That is, management can regulate these expenditures. Failure costs are uncontrollable. Notice in Figure 10.1, as the controllable costs increase, the uncontrollable costs decrease, and vice versa. This would appear to indicate that as more resources are devoted to the appraisal of quality and the prevention of failure, the costs due to failure, both internal and external, decrease. Total quality costs are represented by the uppermost curve in the figure. At some point, the cost of appraising quality and preventing failures equals the cost of failures. At that point, the total quality cost curve is at its lowest level. This point, where the appraisal and prevention cost curve intersects the failure cost curve, is the optimal quality cost.

OBTAINING AND ANALYZING QUALITY COST DATA

Quality costs cannot be analyzed unless the appropriate data are collected and made available. The collection and compilation of these data are generally the responsibility of the accounting department. However, the development of the quality cost information system requires cooperation between the quality control department and accounting. This is particularly true when the quality control data cross traditional departmental lines on which the accounting system may be based.

It is frequently a simple matter to pull the quality cost data together in the desired format. When computerized information systems are used, the collection and compilation of these data are usually simple matters. Quality costs should be compiled by product line, projects, departments or with respect to any operating unit to which control can be applied. In a small business, this could go as low as an individual operator.

Once collected, the quality costs must be analyzed before any action can be taken. The costs by themselves provide insufficient information for analysis. A basis for comparison should be established in order to relate the quality costs to some aspect of the business that is sensitive to change. Some common measurement bases are manufacturing costs, labor costs, unit of product and sales volume.

Quality costs per dollar of manufacturing cost is a common index used in manufacturing operations. Manufacturing costs consist of direct labor, direct material and overhead. These data should be readily available since manufacturing cost accounting systems are practically always in place to gather this information.

Quality costs per dollar of direct labor is another common index. Direct labor information is also readily available from the cost accounting system. In some cases, direct labor hours are used instead of dollars.

Quality costs per unit of product can sometimes be a good comparison base. This index is most useful when the number of product lines are few or are all similar to one another. When the company has many dissimilar product lines, comparisons may be difficult to make and interpret.

Probably the most common type of index applicable to both manufacturing and nonmanufacturing organizations is sales volume, that is, quality costs per sales dollar. Sales are a good indicator of operating level and for wholesale, retail and service operations may be the only practical comparison base.

Once quality cost indexes are determined, that is, quality cost per some comparison base, what can management do with this information? Of course, quality costs should be maintained at an optimal level, that is, at the optimal point on the quality cost curves illustrated in Figure 10.1. These curves are theoretical however and somewhat difficult to relate to the actual costs incurred in some specific operation.

For the manager in some small or medium-sized business, the compilation of quality cost data cannot be a one-shot attempt. It is necessary to compile and analyze these data over a period of time in order to see how the different quality costs relate to one another in that specific operation and to determine where the optimal point actually lies. For that reason, the quality cost index should be maintained for each category of quality costs, that is, prevention and appraisal costs on the one hand and failure costs on the other. Over a period of time, say 6 to 12 months, a quality cost curve similar to Figure 10.1 can be plotted using the data obtained. Keep in mind that management has direct control over prevention and appraisal costs, therefore, failure costs can be determined for various levels of expenditures in the controllable areas. When sufficient data has been compiled over an adequate period of time, it should be possible to determine at least an approximate optimum for quality control expenditures.

Consider the data compiled for Westwind, Inc. over an eight-month period for the months of March through October. The numerical data represent the quality cost index using sales volume as the comparison base. Actually, the quality cost index is expressed as a percent of sales and was obtained by dividing the quality costs by dollars of sales and multiplying the result by 100. These data for the eight months are provided in Table 10.1.

By studying the series of indexes it is apparent that as more effort or expenditures were applied to prevention and appraisal, total quality costs as a percent of sales declined. However, it took about three months before this effect became noticeable. A dramatic reduction in failure costs occurred between the months of June and July. At this point approximately 1.4% to 1.5% of the sales dollar was expended

Table 10.1. Westwind, Incorporated Quality Cost Index (Quality Costs as a % of Sales)

	MARCH	APRIL	MAY	JUNE	JULY	AUG	SEPT	OCT
Prevention and Appraisal Costs	1.7	1.7	2.1	1.7	1.4	1.5	1.5	1.6
Failure Costs	6.9	6.4	7.1	5.3	3.9	3.9	4.1	4.0
Total Quality Costs	8.6	8.1	9.2	7.0	5.3	5.4	5.6	5.6

on prevention and appraisal. For the four months, July through September, with expenditures for prevention and appraisal remaining fairly steady at about 1.5% of sales, failure costs leveled out at approximately 4.0% and total quality costs at about 5.6%. From these data Westwind's management could conclude that expenditures on prevention and appraisal would be optimal at approximately 1.5% of sales, and total quality costs would therefore be at an optimal point of about 5.5% of sales.

Although the optimal figure for quality costs will vary from industry to industry and even from company to company within the same industry, this type of analysis enables management to determine where that point should be.

INSPECTION

In many small businesses, inspection and quality control are virtually synonymous. In those cases the control of quality is exercised by inspecting the product, usually on a 100% basis. In time, more sophisticated quality control techniques are usually adopted, including inspection on a sampling basis. Management is often surprised to find that sampling inspection is often more effective and considerably more economical than 100% inspection. However, inspection, whether 100% or by sampling, is an essential ingredient of any quality control activity and warrants discussion as part of a profit maximization program.

The purpose of inspection is to insure that the standards established for materials, parts and finished product are maintained. Inspection of incoming materials is just as important a part of the quality control process as inspection of outgoing product. Incoming inspection is necessary to assure that defective material does not enter the production process. It is also necessary in order to be sure that the vendor is meeting his contractual obligations regarding the quality of the items purchased. Inspection of outgoing product is essential to assure that defective product does not reach the customer.

The time of inspection varies in part with the nature of materials or products being inspected. Purchased materials and parts are usually inspected when they are received and before they are placed in inventory or sent to the factory for processing. In some cases, materials or products are inspected in the plant of the vendor during or after completion of the manufacturing processes. A dress manufacturer, for example, sometimes contracts with textile mills for the manufacture of special fabrics of a specified weave or pattern. To assure that the materials will be of the desired quality, the dress manufacturer may place an inspector in the plant of the textile mill. A fruit-packing company that contracts to buy the fruit from an orchard may inspect the fruit before it is picked to assure the quality of the fruit and to determine when it should be picked.

Work in process usually cannot be inspected by professional inspectors at every step in production. Usually management establishes certain control points where errors may be detected before serious losses have been incurred. How many control points should be established and which points should be selected will depend upon the nature of the product, the possibility of the concealment of defects because the part is covered by other parts, and the amount of work that may be expended later on defective parts or assemblies. Usually a number of inspections are necessary at different stages in production.

The product is usually inspected when finished. A motor is tested and broken in on a test stand. A washing machine, an electric iron, or an electric fan is connected with power lines at the completion of the assembly operations and its performance checked. Electric fuses and lamps are inspected by trying them in electrical connections. Tin cans and other containers are tested to assure that none have holes. The final inspection frequently serves as a check on the inspectors at earlier stages of production.

STATISTICAL METHODS IN QUALITY CONTROL

In the inspection of many commodities, 100% inspection is not feasible because the cost of complete inspection would be excessive in relation to its advantages. In other cases, complete inspection is impossible because the units inspected are destroyed or made unusable by inspection. For example, when cans of food are opened for inspection in a packing plant, the fruit can no longer be sold. In a glass factory the bottles and jars that are tested in a laboratory are sometimes subjected to increasing weight until they break. Some containers are cut from top to bottom to permit a measurement of the thickness of the glass, and others are broken in the making of tests for stresses and strains in the glass. Other products that may be destroyed in the course of tests for inspection are electric fuses, cartridge caps, and wire tested for tensile strength. In such cases, statistical methods and sampling techniques must be employed.

The application of statistics to quality control generally falls into two major categories. These are *process control* and *acceptance control*. These terms are not entirely descriptive of the functions performed, since the meanings and the functions tend to overlap to some extent. The categories seem to be more clearly defined by a description of the principal tools used in each. For example, the major set of tools used in process control are control charts. The major set of tools used in acceptance control are acceptance sampling plans or simply acceptance samples.

The reader should not conclude that control charts and acceptance sampling are the only statistical techniques used in quality control; however, they are the most common and for the small or medium-sized manufacturer are the most applicable to a profit maximization program.

A process is said to be in control if it operates within certain limits specified numerically in terms of the quality characteristic being measured. When any quality characteristic is being observed or measured, the observed value will vary from observation to observation. Some variation is inevitable and is an inherent part of the process being observed. The acceptable variation inherent to the process is due to a wide range of random causes and is called *random variation*. Variation due to causes that are not part of this random system leads to excessive variation which is not acceptable. Such nonrandom causes of variation are referred to as *assignable causes*. A process which exhibits variation subject to assignable causes is said to be out of control.

Control charts are tools for recording observations made on a process and indicating when the process is apparently out of control. When an out-of-control condition is indicated, the process is stopped, and an attempt is made to locate and eliminate the assignable cause or causes. Since control charts are used to control the quality of continuous processes, their use falls under the general heading of process control.

In contrast to a continuous process, there are situations or stages in many processes when a product is produced or accumulated in finite batches or lots. When a large number of units of a product are gathered into a lot, acceptance sampling is frequently used to determine whether the quality of the lot is good or bad. Of course, the criterion for deciding what constitutes good quality or bad quality must be specified in advance.

Conceivably, the condition of the lot could be determined by examining or inspecting every unit of product in the lot. For large lots, this procedure, which is called 100% inspection, would be very expensive and time-consuming. Acceptance sampling plans provide a method by which a portion of the lot, called a sample, is inspected; and a decision on the lot quality is based on the condition of the sample. Of course, if the sample indicates that the lot is bad, the entire lot must be inspected and the bad product replaced by a good product. This process is called *rectification*. However, if the sample indicates that the lot is good, the entire lot is accepted without further inspection.

To show how statistical quality control techniques are applied in practical situations, a few examples are provided below.

The Excelsior Canning Company is a small food processor with a single plant located in Ohio. Among its various products, Excelsior cans various types of fruit juices which it distributes to supermarkets. One quality characteristic that must be controlled is the net weight. An 8-ounce can should contain 8 ounces of juice and a 16-ounce can should contain 16 ounces. Less than the specified weight cheats the customer, while more than the specified weight is costly to the company.

The cans are filled by an automatic machine on a continuous production line. The machine is adjusted once each day at the beginning of the shift, however, automatic machines have a tendency to drift away from their original settings. Periodic readjustments to the machine settings are costly since they require interrupting the process. The quality control department of Excelsior has established a system of control charts for the process and a procedure by which periodic samples of juice cans are weighed. The average weight of each sample is plotted on the charts. If the process goes out of control and requires a readjustment of the filling machine, the control chart or charts will indicate this condition. By using these charts, unnecessary adjustments are avoided while out-of-control conditions are detected promptly. This is an example of process control.

Accutec, Inc. produces plastic control knobs to a set of specifications for a large manufacturer of television sets. The knobs are used as on-off and volume controls and therefore must fit tightly over a metal shaft that protrudes from the television chassis. If a knob fits too loosely or does not fit at all, the knob is defective and must be scrapped. It is inevitable that some defective knobs are produced by the process, but if the proportion of defective knobs is too high, the company will lose money. A control chart, called a p chart, was established for this process by the quality control department. The purpose of the chart is to indicate an out-of-control condition resulting in the proportion of defective being too high or too low. The latter condition might indicate errors in the inspection process. Either condition could be costly for the company in terms of excessive scrap or an inspection process that fails to detect defective products. This is another example of process control.

Generico Pharmaceuticals produces a medicine for the treatment of high blood pressure. The medicine is contained in gelatin capsules, and the amount of the drug in each capsule must be carefully controlled by weight. The capsules are manufactured in batches or lots of 100,000 capsules, and it would be impractical to weigh each capsule produced. It would also be impractical to weigh individual capsules in a sample, since the scale would not be capable of getting precise weights of such a small item. Instead a plan was established in which a sample of 500 capsules was selected from each lot of 100,000 and weighed all together. An average weight is computed from the sample and compared with certain critical limits previously determined. If the average weight falls within these limits, the lot is accepted. However, if the average falls outside of these limits, the entire lot is rejected. This is an example of acceptance control. Another example of acceptance control is given by the Thermosystems procedure which follows.

Thermosystems, Inc. manufactures a wide variety of heating and cooling systems for residential use. One component common to all of these systems is a thermostatic control switch. These control switches are purchased in large quantities from the Calor Component Company. Each shipment received from Calor contains 5000 control switches. The quality control department of Thermosystems has established an acceptance sampling plan for incoming material. Out of each lot of 5000 control switches a sample of 200 is tested. If eight or more of the switches in the sample fail to work properly, the entire lot is rejected and returned to the vendor. This procedure protects Thermosystems, Inc. against allowing an excessive number of defective control switches from entering its production process.

Process Control

The primary advantage of process control techniques is that advance warning is received when a process is going out of control. By charting values obtained from periodic samples of the process output, the process is monitored continuously. As the sample values indicate a trend toward either control limit or if a value falls outside of a control limit, an immediate adjustment can be made before defective units appear. Should the evaluation of a sample show that the tolerance has been exceeded, a close inspection will have to be made of the output produced between the last two samples to uncover any unsatisfactory units. As a consequence, inspection costs can be held to a minimum. In addition, adjustments need not be made as long as the output remains within the established limits of acceptability. Reducing the interference with the manufacturing process can lead to increased productivity and lower unit costs.

A control chart is simply a graph that reflects the variability of a process variable with respect to time. A typical control chart looks like the graph shown in Figure 10.2. The horizontal axis on the graph represents time. That is, each point on the horizontal axis coincides with observations made on a subgroup that was drawn from the process at a particular point in time. The vertical axis is scaled in terms of the units in which the process variable is measured.

A solid line, called the center line, is drawn horizontally across the chart and represents a standardized or average value. Two dashed lines are also drawn on the chart parallel to the center line, one above it and one below it. These dashed lines represent an upper control limit, usually abbreviated UCL, and a lower control limit, or LCL.

The mathematical formulas and computations for constructing control charts for any specific process need not be discussed at this point. Tables providing factors for computing control chart limits are readily available and a typical table is included in an appendix to this chapter.

A control chart for averages, called an $\overline{X}$ chart, showing a process that is in control is shown in Figure 10.3. An $\overline{X}$ chart indicating an

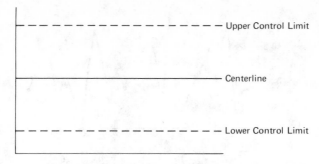

Figure 10.2. A typical control chart.

out-of-control condition is provided in Figure 10.4. The out-of-control condition is indicated by the point falling above the upper control limit.

In controlling some variable quality characteristic of the process, two control charts are usually maintained. The $\overline{X}$ chart illustrated in Figures 10.3 and 10.4 is a chart of sample averages. The R chart is a chart of sample ranges. The range is simply the difference between the largest value in the sample and the smallest. While the $\overline{X}$ chart monitors the centering of the process, the R chart monitors its variability. An out-of-control indication on either chart is an indication that a process adjustment is necessary.

The charts for averages and ranges are called *variables control charts.* A variable refers to a measured characteristic such as a dimension. Often, manufactured items and even documents are simply classified as good or defective depending upon whether or not they meet

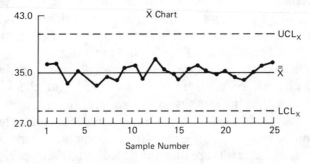

Figure 10.3. An $\overline{X}$ chart showing a process in control.

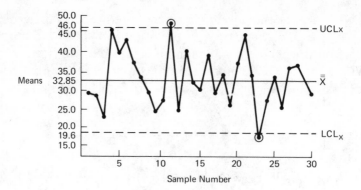

Figure 10.4. An $\overline{X}$ chart showing a process out of control.

all the specifications established for them. When that is the case, an attributes control chart for the proportion defective is used. This is referred to as a *p* chart. The appearance and the use of the *p* chart is similar to the variables charts illustrated. The chart has a center line and an upper and lower control limit. Whenever *p,* the proportion defective, falls outside of one of the limits an out-of-control condition is assumed to exist, and the process is stopped until the cause is determined.

Acceptance Control

Decisions concerning the acceptability of production lots by a determination of the number of defective units in a random sample is known as *acceptance sampling*. The size of the sample is mathematically determined on the basis of a number of factors. Acceptance sampling is often used by a company for the examination of incoming materials, or it may be used within a company as materials move from one department to another. Finally, and most importantly, it is used in the final inspection process before an order is shipped to a customer. Each unit of the sample is inspected and checked to see whether it is within the established tolerances. If so, it is accepted; if not, it is rejected. If the number of rejects in the sample is less than a predetermined quantity, the entire lot is accepted; otherwise it is rejected. Unacceptable lots are then subjected to 100% inspection so the defective units can be eliminated. Complete inspection can be done by the purchaser, or the rejected lots can be returned to the vendor for this purpose. In either case, it is the responsibility of the supplier to make adjustments if a production lot is rejected.

Where there is large volume production, there invariably will be some unsatisfactory units, no matter how stable the manufacturing process. Vendors and purchasers understand that this situation exists. Contracts often contain clauses indicating that an agreement has been reached concerning the matter. Buyers understand that the higher the percentage of defects they are willing to accept, the lower the contract price, because a higher level of quality would result in additional supplier costs.

Most often, there will be an established quality range agreeable to both the vendor and the buyer, rather than a single quality level. The high point is known as the *acceptable quality level* (AQL) which is the smallest percentage of defectives that the supplier can provide under his present manufacturing operations. This is the best quality which can be provided. At the other extreme, the customer states that he will not accept lots that contain more than a certain percentage of unsatisfactory units. This is the low point of the quality range and is called the *lot tolerance percentage defective* (LTPD). Sometimes this value is referred to as the *Rejectable Quality Level* (RQL).

Frequently, the parties to the contract agree to use acceptance sampling inspection and abide by its outcome. Both understand that there are certain risks in this system because the laws of probability do not guarantee complete accuracy and the sample may contain more or less than its share of unacceptable units. On occasion, a good lot will be rejected, causing additional expense for the producer because of the 100% inspection of the lot when it was not really warranted. This is the producer's risk. The purchaser may be accepting a bad lot at times also, and he then bears the additional loss which may arise. This is the purchaser's or consumer's risk.

These risks can be minimized by increasing the sample size. Theoretically, by continuously enlarging the size of the sample until it encompasses the entire production lot, the risks would become continuously smaller so that they would be completely eliminated when the entire production lot was inspected. In practice this would not occur because even 100% inspection does not guarantee complete accuracy. Expanding the sample would lead to increased inspection costs which subvert the purpose of sampling. The savings in inspection costs through the use of sampling benefit both groups and most often offset the aforementioned risks.

The size of the sample to be chosen and the acceptance number, which is the maximum number of unsatisfactory units that can be present in the sample if the lot is to be accepted, are determined mathematically. This statistical computation takes into account four factors: the producer's risk, the consumer's risks, the lowest expected percentage of defectives that the vendor is to supply (acceptable quality level), and the highest percentage of defectives that the purchaser is willing to accept (lot tolerance percentage defective). Tables are available for all combinations of these factors so that the practical application of acceptance sampling does not require statistical knowledge. The most common tables of acceptance sampling plans are provided by the U.S. government and are referred to as Mil-Std-105D.[*]

Acceptance sampling can be undertaken by different types of sampling plans. Decisions to accept or reject a production lot may be based on the results of a single sample, a double sample, or a multiple sample. For each plan, the size of the sample differs and the acceptance number varies. The results of all these plans should provide the same decision and thus the same degree of protection.

Tables such as those found in Mil-Std-105D are extremely easy to use. The sampling plan is determined by the size of the lot subject to sampling inspection and the acceptable quality level or AQL expressed in terms of percent defective. For example, for a lot size of 1000 and a desired AQL of 2.5 percent the sampling plan is designated: $n = 80$, $c = 5$. The letter n represents the size of the sample while the letter c represents the greatest number of defectives allowed. In other words this sampling plan requires that a random sample of 80 units be drawn from the lot of 1000 and inspected. If the sample contains 5 or fewer defectives, the lot is accepted. If the sample contains more than 5 defectives, the entire lot is rejected.

The inspection of 80 units is much more economical than the inspection of the entire lot of 1000. However, there are risks of error in any sampling plan. These risks can also be determined from the manual. For this plan, the producer's risk, that is, the risk of rejecting a good lot, is approximately 1%. The consumer's risk, that is, the risk of ac-

---

[*] Sampling Procedures and Tables for Inspection by Attributes, U.S. Department of Defense, Mil-Std-105D.

cepting a bad lot that contains 11% defective product, is approximately 10%. However, as mentioned previously, even 100% inspection does not guarantee that no errors will be made. In fact, an axiom of quality control states that 100% inspection is only about 80% effective. Consequently, sampling inspection is generally more effective and a great deal more economical than 100% inspection in most instances.

SUMMARY

Without adequate control of the quality of its product, a firm's competitive position is endangered. It is unlikely that the enterprise would survive in a market where quality control is a primary objective of other companies in the industry.

The achievement of a process, which will yield a product considered standard because it conforms to an established range of acceptability, results in many benefits for a concern. Management is able to standardize its operations so that production can proceed with a minimum number of changes and adjustments. The optimum method of production can then be devised, and the workers can become fully trained and experienced in the procedure to provide the desired quality of output. This can lead to a substantial increase in the quantity of production because of the familiarity of the workers with the method of production. There is little need to interrupt the work cycle for unnecessary adjustments.

This best method of production will also bring lower costs of operations. This is primarily true of unit costs, but even total costs of production can be reduced as better equipment and procedures are devised. The number of unacceptable units of output is materially lessened; thus the losses resulting from scrap and additional time and effort to rework defective items, which must be considered in manufacturing costs, are kept at a minimum.

As a company's quality control program brings the aforementioned benefits as well as a better standard quality for its product, the morale of the employees improves. Fewer rejects mean fewer reworks (for which no credit is received) for the workers. This leads to higher wages for the workers and a better record of output for the foremen. This can reflect in improved management-employee relations in other aspects of the industrial environment.

Quality control is of utmost importance in mass production operations. The manufacture of a standard product requires the interchangeability of parts which permits the separation of the machining from the assembling operation. If all of the parts for a particular sequence could not be considered as identical, mass production would not be possible.

APPENDIX TO CHAPTER 10:
APPLICATION OF CONTROL CHARTS

When a quality characteristic of a process is observed as a measurment, variables data result. This does not necessarily mean that the characteristic must be a dimension such as length, width, or diameter. It could be an electrical measurement, a measure of strength, a weight, a measure of acidity called pH or any other quantity that can be measured on a continuous scale. For variables data, control is generally applied to the process average or mean and to the variability of the individual observations about the mean. This means that two separate control charts are required, since any assignable cause could affect either the process mean, its variability, or both. Consequently, an $\overline{X}$ chart is used to plot the means of samples, while a separate chart is used to plot some measure of the variability that occurs within each sample. This measure of variability within the sample can be either the sample standard deviation, σ or the sample range, R. Both of these statistics can be used as an estimator of the process standard deviation σ' which is a measure of the process variability.

Two charts, usually an $\overline{X}$ and R chart, are used together to control a variable characteristic for several reasons. First, the mean of a process may change while the variability remains the same. An example of this situation would occur if an automatic machine had a tendency to drift away from its original setting. Such a condition would show up on the $\overline{X}$ chart but would not be reflected on an R chart. On the other hand, the variability of the process could change without affecting the mean. A change of operators on a machine tool could cause this situation to occur. A change of this type would affect the R chart but might not appear on the $\overline{X}$ chart.

Control limits for the $\overline{X}$ chart are based on the mean plus and minus three standard errors of the mean. That is

$$\overline{X}' \pm 3\sigma_{\overline{x}}$$

where $\sigma_{\overline{x}} = \sigma'/\sqrt{n}$ is the standard error of the mean, a measure of the way the sample means vary. The value $\overline{X}'$ becomes the center line on the control chart. This represents a true or *standardized* value of the process mean. By a standardized value we mean a value established as a standard. If a standardized value has not been established then the mean or average of the sample means, called $\overline{\overline{X}}$, is used where

$$\overline{\overline{X}} = \frac{\Sigma \overline{x}}{k}$$

The letter k represents the number of sample means used and Σ simply represents the sum.

Since $\sigma_{\overline{x}}$ is based on a known or estimated value of σ' (the process standard deviation), an estimate can be obtained from the average range of the samples called $\overline{R}$ as follows:

$$\overline{R} = \frac{\Sigma R_i}{k}$$

where k = the number of sample ranges and Σ again means sum. Then σ' is estimated from the factor d_2 which is given in Table 10.2 as follows:

$$\sigma' = \overline{R}/d_2$$

Control limits on the R chart are also based upon the average value of the statistic, $\overline{R}$, plus and minus three standard errors of the statistic. That is, control limits on the R chart are based on

$$\overline{R} \pm 3\sigma_R$$

Fortunately for most quality control practitioners, it is not necessary to compute the standard errors of the mean or the range. Factors have already been computed for the purpose of determining control limits for the various variables control charts. These factors

Table 10.2. Factors for Estimating σ' from $\overline{R}$

SUBGROUP SIZE n	d_2
2	1.128
3	1.693
4	2.059
5	2.326
6	2.534
7	2.704
8	2.847
9	2.970
10	3.078
11	3.173
12	3.258
13	3.336
14	3.407
15	3.472
16	3.532
17	3.588
18	3.640
19	3.689
20	3.735
25	3.931
30	4.086

for various subgroup sizes, can be found in Table 10.3. Their application is summarized as follows:

$\overline{X}$ CHART	CENTER LINE	USE FACTOR	LCL	UCL
1. σ' assumed known	$\overline{X}'$ or $\overline{\overline{X}}$	A	$\overline{X}' - A\sigma'$	$\overline{X}' + A\sigma'$
2. $\overline{R}$ for estimating σ'	$\overline{X}'$ or $\overline{\overline{X}}$	A_2	$\overline{X}' - A_2\overline{R}$	$\overline{X}' + A_2\overline{R}$

R CHART	CENTER LINE	USE FACTOR	LCL	UCL
1. σ' assumed known	$\overline{R} = d_2\sigma'$	D_1 and D_2	$D_1\sigma'$	$D_2\sigma'$
2. $\overline{R}$ for estimating σ'	$\overline{R}$	D_3 and D_4	$D_3\overline{R}$	$D_4\overline{R}$

Referring to the Table 10.3 notice that for small subgroups, the factors D_1, and D_3 are equal to zero. This means that for these subgroup sizes, the lower control limit on the R chart will always be zero.

As an example, values of measurements of a process variable are re-

Table 10.3. Factors for Computing Control Chart Lines

NUMBER OF OBSERVA-TIONS IN SAMPLE, n	CHART FOR AVERAGES					CHART FOR RANGES				
	FACTORS FOR CONTROL LIMITS			FACTORS FOR CENTRAL LINE			FACTORS FOR CONTROL LIMITS			
	A	A_1	A_2	d_2	$1/d_2$	d_3	D_1	D_2	D_3	D_4
2	2.121	3.760	1.880	1.128	0.8865	0.853	0	3.686	0	3.267
3	1.732	2.394	1.023	1.693	0.5907	0.838	0	4.353	0	2.575
4	1.500	1.880	0.729	2.059	0.4857	0.880	0	4.698	0	2.282
5	1.342	1.596	0.577	2.382	0.4299	0.864	0	4.918	0	2.115
6	1.225	1.410	0.483	2.534	0.3945	0.848	0	5.078	0	2.004
7	1.134	1.277	0.419	2.704	0.3698	0.833	0.205	5.203	0.076	1.924
8	1.061	1.175	0.373	2.847	0.3512	0.829	0.387	5.307	0.136	1.864
9	1.000	1.094	0.337	2.970	0.3367	0.803	0.546	5.394	0.164	1.816
10	0.949	1.028	0.308	3.078	0.3249	0.797	0.687	5.469	0.223	1.777
11	0.905	0.973	0.285	3.173	0.3152	0.787	0.812	5.534	0.258	1.744
12	0.865	0.925	0.266	3.258	0.3069	0.778	0.924	5.592	0.284	1.716
13	0.832	0.884	0.249	3.336	0.2993	0.770	1.026	5.646	0.308	1.692
14	0.802	0.848	0.235	3.407	0.2935	0.762	1.121	5.693	0.329	1.671
15	0.775	0.816	0.223	3.472	0.2880	0.755	1.207	5.737	0.348	1.652
16	0.750	0.788	0.212	3.532	0.2831	0.749	1.285	5.779	0.364	1.635
17	0.728	0.762	0.203	3.588	0.2787	0.743	1.359	5.817	0.379	1.621
18	0.707	0.735	0.194	3.640	0.2747	0.739	1.426	5.854	0.392	1.608
19	0.688	0.717	0.187	3.689	0.2711	0.733	1.490	5.888	0.404	1.596
20	0.671	0.697	0.180	3.735	0.2677	0.723	1.548	5.922	0.414	1.586
21	0.655	0.679	0.173	3.778	0.2647	0.724	1.606	5.950	0.425	1.576
22	0.640	0.662	0.167	3.819	0.2618	0.720	1.659	5.979	0.434	1.566
23	0.626	0.647	0.162	3.858	0.2582	0.716	1.710	6.006	0.443	1.557
24	0.612	0.632	0.157	3.895	0.2567	0.712	1.759	6.031	0.452	1.548
25	0.600	0.619	0.153	3.931	0.2544	0.709	1.804	6.058	0.459	1.541
Over 25		$\sqrt{n}$	$\sqrt{n}$							

corded below for 25 samples of $n = 6$. The mean and range of each sample is given.

For the $\overline{X}$ chart, the center line is placed at

$$\overline{\overline{X}} = 35.02.$$

The control limits are based on $\overline{\overline{X}} \pm A_2 \overline{R}$. The factor A_2 for samples of size 6 is obtained from Table 10.3. $A_2 = 0.483$. The upper and lower control limits are

SAMPLE NUMBER	$\overline{X}$	R
1	35.7	11.7
2	36.4	13.0
3	33.2	13.2
4	35.2	11.4
5	35.0	12.0
6	32.7	10.2
7	34.4	13.3
8	33.8	14.3
9	35.6	12.8
10	35.9	12.4
11	34.0	12.3
12	37.1	12.8
13	35.3	10.7
14	34.9	14.5
15	34.0	10.2
16	35.6	10.6
17	36.2	9.9
18	35.2	13.8
19	35.0	13.2
20	35.1	15.0
21	34.4	12.8
22	33.9	11.9
23	35.0	10.9
24	35.8	12.9
25	36.1	13.7
Totals	875.5	312.5

$$\overline{\overline{X}} = \frac{875.5}{25} = 35.02$$

$$\overline{R} = \frac{312.5}{25} = 12.5$$

$$35.02 \pm (0.483)(12.5)$$

or

$$UCL = 41.05$$
$$LCL = 28.98$$

For the R chart, the center line is placed at

$$\overline{R} = 12.5$$

The control limits are based on factors D_4 and D_3 as follows:

$$UCL = D_4 \overline{R}$$
$$LCL = D_3 \overline{R}.$$

From Table 10.3, $D_4 = 2.004$ and $D_3 = 0$. Therefore

$$UCL = (2.004)(12.5) = 25.5$$
$$LCL = (0)(12.5) = 0$$

11. Cost and Budgetary Control

We have emphasized the fact that the primary purpose of any business is to make a profit. Without profits, the business organization cannot survive for very long. We have also indicated that simply showing some profit during an operating period is not in itself sufficient for survival, particularly in a competitive economy. The firm should maximize profits.

Profit is a financial surplus which results when the income from the sale of a product or service exceeds the cost of producing it. Consequently there are two primary factors involved in profit: the price at which the product or service can be sold in a competitive marketplace and the cost of producing it. In terms of the two factors, price and cost, the question of control is important.

A company may sometimes be able to control the selling price of its product or service, however, in most cases the price is generally determined by the market. In the medium-to-long run, competitors, producers of substitute products or services, and customers determine the price. Consequently, management does not usually have control, at least not total control, of the price of its product. Management does, or should, however have control over the costs of production. Profits or losses are determined in the area of costs, and therefore control of costs is essential to profit maximization. The reader should note that the techniques and procedures discussed in previous chapters were basically techniques for minimizing costs.

Before management can exercise control over costs, adequate cost data must be available. When cost records are provided to management, comparisons can be made with cost standards based on various management techniques such as work simplification programs, time studies and plant layout. When excessive costs are present it is necessary to determine why and to provide corrective action in order to minimize the problems. This is cost control.

The acquisition of cost data is of primary importance in a firm. Management needs all cost information relative to operations for proper control. Cost accounting systems provide the means for determining the unit cost of production. Although primarily developed for manufacturing operations, the cost accounting concept should be applicable to sales and service businesses as well. Since there are two basic manufacturing processes, each has a different cost accounting system. One is the process cost system which is used for continuous manufacturing; the other is the production order or job lot cost system which is used in diversified manufacturing.

The process cost system is used to determine the total cost of operating each department or each process in manufacturing. The average cost at each stage of production can then be determined by dividing the cost of operating the department by the number of units produced. Total average cost per unit is determined by adding the average costs at the various stages of production or the average costs in each department. Examples of this type of production are the refining of sugar and the mass production of television sets.

The production-order cost system is used when there is diversified manufacturing. All costs relative to each production order are placed together under this system, so that the cost of each unit or each order can be determined. This type of cost system is applicable to job shop or custom production. It is especially suited for firms that manufacture high-cost products to customer order. However, it is also used by firms that manufacture large quantities of relatively low-cost product to customer order.

Because of the simplicity of the process cost system and the relative complexity of the production-order cost system, this discussion will concentrate on the latter. In continuous manufacturing, costs tend to be stable because continuous production processes do not change often.

There are two major types of production-order cost systems. These are the *historical cost system* and the *standard cost system*. A historical cost system shows the actual costs for some present or preceding period. A standard cost system shows cost based on some predetermined standard and the amount by which the actual cost varies from the standard.

Cost accounting attempts to determine the actual cost of manufacturing or producing the product or products of the firm. There are essentially three major categories of manufacturing cost: direct material, direct labor and overhead.

Direct materials are the costs of materials that become part of the finished product. The identity and amount of these materials are relatively easy to determine and identify with the product. The cost of the materials used is simply charged to the order in which they are used.

The cost of direct materials can be determined from the materials requisitions which originate from production control. These requisitions list the amount of materials to be issued to each specific production order. The record of the issuance of this material is sent to the cost accounting department.

Direct labor refers to wages paid to the workers who transform the raw material into the finished product. Again, the direct labor cost associated with each order is easily determined. Direct labor costs are computed from the time cards issued for each operation listed on the manufacturing order. The calculations are quickly made as the starting and completion times and the labor grade which did the work are recorded on each card. These cards must also pass through the cost accounting department.

The difficulties in determining cost usually arise in allocating indirect or overhead expense. These are all the other costs not directly related to the manufactured product itself. These costs can also generally be divided into the three categories of manufacturing expense, administrative expense and selling expense.

Administrative expenses include all office costs such as executive and clerical salaries, rent, and office supplies, while sales expense includes all of the costs of marketing the product such as advertising, salesmen's salaries, warehousing of finished goods and shipping expense. Even though some of these administrative and selling expenses can be identified with a particular production order, they are generally grouped with the administrative or the selling costs.

Manufacturing expense or factory overhead consists of all costs incurred in the production of a product other than direct materials and direct labor. These costs cannot be assigned to any single job, lot or product, but are required for the general operation of the plant or for some particular department. These costs would include indirect materials or supplies used to facilitate the manufacturing processes; indirect labor which is utilized in the factory but does not work on the product, such as salaries for foremen and maintenance and materials handling personnel; the wear and tear on the building and machines, known as depreciation; and interest, rent, taxes, power and light. These indirect manufacturing expenses must be apportioned to each unit of product manufactured.

Overhead is distributed so that each unit produced will carry its proportionate share of these expenses and the total cost of the product can be determined. The allocation procedure involves two steps: first, the assignment of overhead expenses to the manufacturing departments, and then, the prorating of the departmental overhead to the product or products. If the distribution of overhead is inaccurate the result can be the overpricing or underpricing of the product. Either could prove disastrous for the firm. Overpricing can lead to lost sales and revenues while underpricing may cause direct loss on the units sold. Both result in profit erosion.

There is no single, correct and most accurate method for distributing overhead. It is the responsibility of management to adopt a system that can be administered effectively and that will provide an accurate allocation.

All of the costs previously mentioned under manufacturing overhead can be divided into two categories: controllable and noncontrollable costs. The manager should give his attention to those costs which are controllable to see that the most efficient utilization is secured. Controllable costs include supplies, maintenance costs and power. He can do nothing about noncontrollable costs because they are contractual arrangements and have no relationship to production. These include rent, interest and taxes. Although depreciation of buildings and machines are not contractual items, they also are noncontrollable costs since obsolescence which enters into depreciation has no relationship to the amount of production.

STANDARD COSTS

A standard cost system establishes costs for direct materials, direct labor and overhead for a specified volume of production.

Before standard direct material costs can be provided, a study of the type, quality, quantity and price must be made. The type, quality and quantity of materials that will be needed are determined by the product engineers. Material price is based on the average of costs and adjusted for short-run changes in either direction. Management will take the engineering and purchasing departments' studies, provide a necessary allowance for scrap, waste or shrinkage, and furnish this information to the cost accounting department for the establishment of a standard direct material cost.

Even more background preparation is necessary before standard direct labor cost can be established. This calls for the standardization of all working conditions at their most efficient level. Included are plant layout, the operating condition of the machines and equipment, and materials handling. Work simplification and time studies should be completed also. The workers must be aware of these conditions and be properly trained to do the required work in the most satisfactory manner. Wage rates must be established for each labor grade and the highest labor grade which should be assigned to an operation should be specified. With all of these data the standard direct labor cost for each operation can be established.

Finally, each production order must bear its proportionate share of overhead. A normal volume of output is determined by management and used for determining the standard overhead cost to be charged to each production unit. The normal volume is basically an average figure based on performance over a representative period of time and adjusted according to forecasts of future activity.

COST CONTROL

The usefulness of cost information depends largely upon the extent to which it is used to reduce, limit, or otherwise control the various activities of the business which give rise to reduced or increased cost. A program for cost control requires an analysis of the data as compiled by the cost accounting department, an interpretation of the significance of the data under existing circumstances, and the development of methods of reducing those activities and those elements of cost believed to be excessive.

Because the cost figures show the costs for materials, labor and manufacturing expenses, each element of cost will require attention. The difficulty may arise from poor management or control of any of the activities that have been discussed in preceding chapters. Difficulties may also result from ineffective organization or a lack of motivation and leadership. Excessive cost might also be due to ineffective staff work, or the duplication of staff services. Low volume of production and sales might be due to poor design of the product, ineffective sales promotion or other causes. Management needs standards in the fields of materials, labor, and expenses for purposes of control. There are no easy solutions to these problems, but continuous attention is required.

Cost control is the function of the line organization. Responsibility for it resides with top management, although authority to exercise control is delegated to all of the subordinate management levels.

An essential component of cost control is adequate financial records and the frequent preparation of summary reports. This includes all of the accounting activities of the enterprise. Responsibility for these activities is usually placed under the controller.

The major objective of cost control is to reduce manufacturing costs. While cost control may effect cost reductions, management may find that in some cases it has achieved nothing by the introduction of a cost control program or by giving it greater emphasis. The difficulty most often is not in the cost control system itself but in the manner in which it is administered by management.

The failure of a cost control program may be due to technical errors within the system. The cause of the failure may be attributed to the improper way the cost control program is used or may result from the use of a cost control system which has been successful elsewhere but is not adapted to the company's needs. These are the least difficult to correct.

The human relations problems that arise from cost control procedures cannot be corrected so quickly. These arise when management fails to secure the cooperation of the lower levels of management (primarily the foremen) and the employees at the time the program is initiated. Problems occur because management often does not concern itself with the effect of such a program on its employees. Most of these difficulties can be overcome if management understands the problems that could arise and exercises its leadership role effectively.

BUDGETARY CONTROL

The budget is a coordinated financial plan for a business. It is basd on estimates of sales, production, purchases, costs and expenses. The purpose of the budget is to plan and control the activities of the business.

The budget represents an important management tool. When budget estimates are formulated, a general view should be taken of all of the activities of the business for the purpose of maintaining a proper balance of activities. When funds are granted or denied for any purpose, the decision is then made that a particular activity is or is not necessary. The increase or decrease in the budget allowance of a department means that the activities of that department will be expanded or curtailed. Since the budget may include expense allowances for all departments, it reflects the views of management concerning the value of each activity and the success of each manager or department head.

The budget emphasizes the idea that expenditures for any purpose should be justified by increased income, decreased expenses, increased tangible or intangible assets, or other business advantages. The business budget reflects management plans and also serves as an important check on management decisions.

The preparation of a budget requires a great deal of communication among the various departments. The final draft represents a plan for the integration of the activities of all departments within the organization. Although a budget is usually expressed in terms of income and expense, it must be developed initially in terms of volume of sales and production, or the amount of activity within a department. The budget is a plan of action which is based partially on past experience, present capabilities and future conditions. The specific period of time covered varies; it may be from one month to several years. The budget also serves as the basis for the allocation of funds. Each department is authorized to spend funds within the limitations established by budget figures.

There are two primary types of budgets: the fixed budget and the variable budget. The fixed budget is based on one level of production. All income and expense figures are computed for this volume of output. A variable budget is actually a set of budgets each one prepared for a different level of output.

The fixed budget has not worked well in industry because few businesses are so stable that sales income and production can be forecast with absolute accuracy. When actual sales and production differ from what has been forecast, the entire budget must be revised. Since the fixed budget is not subject to variation for a definite time period, difficulties arise because of its inflexibility. If more funds are needed because of increased sales, a department might not be able to secure them because they were not authorized by the budget. Likewise, if sales do not warrant further expenditures by a department, it is often difficult to reduce the funds available. Each deviation requires a complete budget revision. However, the fixed budget has been found useful for planning and authorizing expenditures in areas not directly affected by market conditions. Some of these would be research, advertising, plant expansion and capital expenditures.

With several sets of income and cost data for different levels of sales and production, management can be prepared for changes which market conditions may cause. The planning of the operations for all departments can be adjusted to the changed conditions with minimum difficulty. Necessary changes do not result in the confusion or incorrect decisions which are often made too hurriedly.

Some companies may have frequent variations in production. By knowing the expected production, the budget which corresponds to it can be used for that period and then changed if production in the next period is different.

It is only necessary to consider the variable costs in making these alternate budgets since they change in direct proportion to the changes in production. Fixed costs remain constant at all levels of production. Because of the fixed-cost relationship to total output, variable budgets exhibit superior characteristics since fixed costs per unit change at different levels of production. This appears in the variable budgets but is not clearly evidenced by the fixed budgets since only one budget is prepared and comparisons cannot be made.

From the information provided by budgets, an estimated balance sheet and profit and loss statement can be prepared which will show the expected financial position of the company. This is called the master budget.

The preparation of the budget is however only a first step in budgetary control. As with any other control device, comparisons of plans with actual performance and prompt action to correct the deviations are necessary. By comparing its actual operations at periodic intervals with the predetermined operations which appear in the budget, management will be able to determine whether it is ahead of, equal to, or behind what had been planned. The administration of the budget in this manner gives rise to budget control. The comparison of the actual operations with the projected operations is the first phase of budget control. Should actual operations differ from the budget, analysis by management attempts to discern the reasons for the disparity, and then to undertake the necessary corrective measures to eliminate the difference.

It is important that variations between the actual performance and the planned operations be uncovered as soon as possible. The preparation of reports summarizing this information is imperative. In order to accomplish budget control, reports should be provided frequently. Budget deviations which can have a major effect on the company's profit position are given immediate attention even though the variation may be small. Direct labor should be examined on a daily basis, and any discrepancies can immediately be brought under management scrutiny and given the necessary attention before they become too large. Other factors would be considered in some order of priority based on their effect on the company's profit rather than the extent of the divergence of the actual from the budgeted figures.

The use of a budget has many benefits in profit maximization. By planning company operations, it is possible to keep a proper balance among its various departments. Funds do not go into unnecessary expansion or projects or for the unnecessary use of any department. Cooperation between departments is improved as each becomes aware of the goals established for it and how each fits into the overall operation.

Advance planning permits probable difficulties to be foreseen and discussed in advance. They can then be minimized as much as possible, resulting in more efficient operations and more effective utilization of the production factors. Hasty emergency action becomes unnecessary. Managers can make better decisions, as all the necessary information is available and the environment is conducive to effective decision making.

The use of budgets is also advantageous in the implementation of sound organization principles. Planning a budget necessitates a clear division of responsibilities and provides for the delegation of authority to the various management levels in specific departments in order to carry out the operations effectively. The budget promotes the use of the exception principle, as the efforts of a manager can be concentrated on problems that arise without losing time examining operations that do not require attention.

Since the budget establishes definite goals, top management can rate its subordinates on how satisfactorily they have met the predetermined standards. This is possible at all levels of management when the individual budgets are in sufficient detail.

Although the budgetary process will vary from business to business a few guidelines can be established that should be common to all types of business organizations. The budget period is usually one year to coincide with the fiscal year of the organization. Of course there is no rule that says that budgets cannot be established for shorter periods or even longer ones. The period should however cover at least one seasonal cycle if one exists. Some firms continuously revise their budget for the next twelve months. At the end of each month the performance is reviewed, the current month is dropped and an additional month is added. This provides an almost continuous budget review and prohibits expenditures from deviating too sharply from what has been budgeted.

The responsibility for the preparation of the budget estimates and for the operation of the budget varies according to the size and the circumstances of the individual company. The manager should assume ultimate responsibility for the estimates, although he need not attend to all of the details. He should be well informed about every activity of the company and should know the functions of every department and the qualifications of his subordinates. He should also be able to coordinate the conflicting interests of the various departments.

A subordinate directly responsible to the manager is usually placed in charge of the procedure for the development of the budget. This person is usually the controller or the treasurer; but he may hold a position especially created for the budgetary work, such as budget supervisor or budget director. The budget officer may be assisted by a budget committee composed of supervisors who are thoroughly familiar with conditions in the operating departments. This budget committee is usually composed of the heads of the major departments.

The entire organization should take an interest in the preparation and operation of the budget. This condition cannot be created as soon as the budget program is initiated, but results from long and successful experience. A gradual introduction of a budgeting program is frequently advised in order that general participation and interest may be developed.

PREPARATION OF THE BUDGET

Before any estimates are made, the budget committee should meet for a discussion of past performance of the business, prospects during the coming year, and changes in the plans for the business. The head of each department should then prepare and submit to the chief budgetary officer the proposed budget for his department. The budget officer should then combine and summarize the estimates to show the total result. He then sends them to the budget committee together with information to assist the committee in evaluating the proposed program. When the estimates have been revised or approved by the committee, they become the budget for the ensuing period; and they are sent by the budgetary officer to the various departments for their guidance. Any later revisions are recommended by the budget officer and the budget committee.

The proposed budget is assembled for submission to the budget committee as determined by the chief budgetary officer. The expense estimates for each department should be classified by the nature of the expense such as wages, supplies, communication, repairs and maintenance, and taxes. Each department should submit its estimates in terms of dollars and cents. In addition, some departments should submit estimates in terms of physical units such as units of product to be sold, units produced and volume of purchases. The labor budget should show labor costs in dollars and also the number of persons to be employed.

The various estimates are closely related to each other and should be integrated to form a consistent, balanced program. For example, the sales estimate is limited by the amount of the product that can be manufactured; and the amount to be manufactured depends upon the amount that can be sold at a profit. Both the sales and the production budgets may depend upon the funds available for financing and the amount of materials that can be purchased. Expenses vary with the rate of production, although they may not increase or decrease in proportion to changes in the volume of output.

Although the budget is prepared under the supervision of the controller or other budget officer, the control that is exercised through the budget is vested in the operating executives. At times, the controller might seem to be controlling the work of the line and limiting its activities. However, as budget officer, he merely performs a staff or facilitating service, and such authority as he exercises is vested in him as a representative of the chief executive. As the chief accounting officer, he possesses a vast amount of knowledge of the activities of the company, and he may be able to present figures and schedules of income, costs, and expenses within a short time after the need has arisen. In many instances where the controller seems to have power to deny departmental requests for appropriations, he merely acts as advisor to the manager.

When properly prepared and administered the budget is a useful tool for management and should be a vital part of profit maximization. It facilitates planning and provides an instrument for review and control of operations. Management errors can be detected and corrected quickly and expeditiously. However, budgets are not always successful. Usually the failure of budget programs is due to poor management. The difficulty arises when too much is expected in too short a time. The preparation of the budget requires time and effort on the part of the participating department heads. In preparing budget estimates it is not sufficient to simply take last year's figures and adjust them slightly to make them look reasonable. Budget estimates should be based on realistic forecasts transformed into reasonable operating projections and plans for each department and for the business as a whole. The effective use of the budget as a control device depends on the wholehearted cooperation of everyone involved in the process.

SUMMARY

Cost and budgetary control are complementary procedures for obtaining, analyzing and controlling the costs of operating the business. Without accurate cost information, control of costs and realistic budgets are impossible. Without that information and without the control mechanisms established, profit maximization would be impossible. However, a program of cost control and budgetary control in conjunction with the techniques discussed previously can make the difference between an efficiently operated business that is maximizing its profit potential and one in which profit erosion is seriously crippling the organization.

12. Human Resource Management

It is probably a cliché to say that the most important resource of any organization is the human resource. None of the profit maximization techniques described in these pages and no computer system can make a business successful in the absence of a well-trained, conscientious and competent work force. This is true whether the organization is involved in manufacturing or in providing a service. Fortunately, in recent years most managers have recognized these facts regarding the human elements in the organization. Nevertheless, a program of profit maximizatin would not be complete without some attention being devoted to the human resources of the organization.

The major issues in human resource management are straightforward. They include staffing and training, job design, wages and benefits, and the quality of life in the workplace. The last issue has been receiving considerable attention recently. Worker dissatisfaction with the quality of their working lives is apparently one of the major causes of declining quality of output, increasing absenteeism, waste and worker turnover in the United States. Studies of management practices in other countries, particularly Japan and Sweden, have indicated, although not yet conclusively, that different approaches to management may have definite benefits in increasing productivity and improving the quality of output. In any event, the evaluation of the working environment and the worker's attitude toward his job demands attention from the manager who is concerned about profit maximization. Consequently, we will consider each of these issues briefly.

STAFFING AND TRAINING

A growing organization has a continuous need for new employees to staff positions in the expanding business. Even if growth is slow or nonexistent for the time being, requirements for new workers result from natural attrition of the work force due to retirements, terminations, resignations, accidents or death. To avoid labor shortages that can result in understaffing and production delays, the organization must have a source or pool of applicants upon which to draw. It is much better to have a number of applicants to select from than to have none at all when a vacancy occurs.

Because of the importance of developing sources of prospective employees and the eventual selection and training of new employees, the personnel function should be assigned to a particular individual or if activity warrants to a personnel department. Before the personnel function warrants departmentalization, supervisors or department heads have to locate and select workers for their departments. Since they do not undertake this function often, the supervisor does not gain sufficient experience to perform it satisfactorily. In many instances, supervisors do not have the time necessary to make it successful since their other responsibilities require their major attention. The consolidation of the personnel function makes possible an overall picture of the firm's requirements, and workers can be placed in positions which best utilize their capabilities.

The development of sources of applicants is the first step in the process of employee selection. The personnel manager begins his selection of new employees by soliciting applications through his preferred sources. These sources of applicants can be within the company or external to it. Internal sources are often the best. This refers to the filling of a vacancy by the transfer or promotion of another employee. When this is not possible external sources must be used. These external sources include advertising, public and private employment agencies, recruitment at college campuses, job fairs, etc.

Although external recruiting may provide a substantial pool of applicants, not all of these persons will make satisfactory employees. It is through the selection process that the personnel department attempts to find the right person for the right job. Since cost is just as important a consideration in staffing as in any other phase of the operation, it is essential that a selection procedure be developed which will provide, at the least cost, the best worker from those who have applied.

A selection process which can provide workers capable of performing their duties adequately as well as being interested in their jobs can be the basis of a cost advantage for one company over its competitors.

These employees will produce more with less training, supervision, and waste and will become more experienced as they remain at their jobs. All of these things result in lower unit costs of manufacturing and better quality of production.

On the other hand, a poor selection process can become a serious handicap to the company. In the case of unionized work forces, it is often difficult to discharge an employee for inefficiency once he has been hired. Even in nonunion companies, significant damage can be caused by an inefficient or incompetent employee before he can be removed from the job or have his employment terminated.

Techniques and devices for selecting workers are not expected to always result in the employment of applicants who will succeed and the rejection of those who would fail if employed. Employment methods cannot always be expected to rank or to grade workers in a manner predictive of their degree of success on the job. While much progress has been made in the development of scientific methods of selection, no single method or combination of methods can be relied upon to make the best selection in every single case. Employment methods can be considered good if they make possible the classification of applicants into three groups: those likely to succeed on the job, those likely to fail, and those whose success is doubtful.

Since few employers rely upon one technique, a combination of methods is usually used. The following are possible:

    Letter of application
    Interviews
    Psychological tests
    Intelligence tests
    Aptitude tests
    Trade tests
    Recommendations and references

The selection process has not been perfected to determine perfectly the degree of qualification of a potential applicant for a particular job. Even the most satisfactory procedure will sometimes lead to the rejection of some who would make acceptable workers. Unnecessary rejections may never be completely eliminated, but personnel managers should always try to improve their selection techniques. If they are improved, the number of good applicants declared unacceptable will be reduced and the number of unsatisfactory workers accepted should decline.

No single selection technique should be considered wholly reliable in determining the suitability or unsuitability of an applicant. Recognition of the possible deficiencies in each of the various selection methods makes it advisable to use as many as possible without placing complete reliance on any single one. Each technique should supplement the others. Although each will have some imperfections, each should assist in the development of information which can show a general pattern. The judgment of the management personnel responsible for this activity can then be tempered by the results of the selection process. It should not be inferred that the selection process should supplant judgment, because it is exactly this characteristic of management which is basic to all business decisions.

When an applicant is hired he may not be capable of immediately performing the duties of the position he was selected to fill. Some training will likely be required. Of course, there will be instances where a new employee will be experienced in the exact skills required for his new position. In such a case, training, at least formal training, will not be necessary.

However, a company whose policy restricts the selection process to a consideration of only skilled and experienced applicants may discover that this will also create some difficulties. In a normal business period, it may take a long time before skilled workers can be found. In a period of great business activity, it may be virtually impossible. A policy of hiring only skilled workers can result in a labor shortage and lead to reduced production. There would be a greater probability of finding persons possessing the minimum requirements for the job and bringing them up to an adequate skill level through training. In that way, labor shortages and production delays can be minimized.

The value of a good training program is obvious. A company can remain abreast of changing conditions by retraining its present workforce, or it can keep pace with the rapid growth of the business by training its employees to accept greater responsibilities. Properly trained workers are usually more productive. Better quality work is also a result of training. A reduced accident rate also frequently occurs. These results can lead to lower production costs which can assist the company in securing some competitive advantage. Workers also profit through proper training. They become proficient more rapidly and thus are able to earn better wages in a shorter period. Increased production and the improved quality of their work permit them to earn larger paychecks. Advancement is more rapid. All this results in better worker attitudes toward themselves and the company. As their capabilities improve they become more valuable to the company.

Most training in business organizations is essentially on-the-job training. The responsibility of training the new employee on the job rests with his immediate supervisor. However, some companies have established *vestibule training programs*. This is the name given to a training program which is provided to new employees before they are put on the job. The location for this training is completely separate from the actual production operations, hence the name *vestibule* since the worker passes through this training section before going to his assigned department. However, this type of training is used primarily by large companies with a continuous demand for skilled or semi-skilled workers or those that are expanding their operations. These companies have a high degree of specialization of labor and are interested in training workers for specific tasks as rapidly as possible.

When a supervisor is responsible for the on-the-job training of an employee, the personnel department should assist him by providing the services which he requires. This also includes any special training materials or equipment that the supervisor believes are necessary or would be helpful. From time to time the personnel department should evaluate the training programs and their results and provide suggestions for improving the training procedures.

JOB DESIGN

Before an employee can be hired to perform a specific function or to fill a position, the job itself must be clearly defined. This is generally done in the form of a job description.

The job description states in clearly understood terms, the content of the job. Precise language is essential so that the job description will give a complete and exact record of the duties and responsibilities of the job rather than general statements which may be unclear or misinterpreted.

Job descriptions include duties, conditions of work and the requirements of each job. The job description usually follows a prescribed form in order that all essential information may be included. It shows for each job such information as the following:

- The job title;
- The department or location in which the work is performed;
- A complete statement of the various duties performed, and the percentage of the employee time devoted to each type or work;
- The number of persons supervised by the employee, if any, and the extent of the supervision exercised;
- The amount of supervision received and the nature of the supervision;
- Equipment used on the job;
- The relation of the job to other operations;
- The material used on the job;
- Reports and records prepared by the worker;
- Initiative and ingenuity required;
- Personal qualifications of the worker, such as sex, age, education, etc.;
- Effort required such as stooping, standing, pulling, lifting, pushing or sitting;
- Mental requirements such as ability to read and write, add and subtract, read blueprints, or use a slide rule or calculator;
- Physical requirements such as hearing, sight, strength and righthandedness;
- Length of time required to learn the job;
- Experience required;
- Wage or salary range for the job.

The purpose of precisely defining and describing each job or position within the organization is straightforward. Without such a detailed description it would be difficult to hire, train and compensate an employee properly. The factor of compensation is important. Not only must the wage or salary associated with a job be commensurate with the skills, duties, and responsibilities required in order to avoid employee dissatisfaction, it also must be competitive to the wages and salaries paid by other companies attempting to hire people to fill similar positions. Furthermore, jobs that require the same or similar skills, duties, and responsibility within the organization should receive equal compensation. This of course leads to the issue of compensation and benefits that will be discussed below. However, before addressing the compensation structure of the firm the design and evaluation of jobs must be considered.

In order to design or evaluate a job we must first determine exactly what is meant by that term and how a job differs from a task or a position. The word *task* refers to a single activity performed by a worker. When the number of tasks become so large that a single worker cannot perform them all, another worker can be hired and a new *position* is created. A group of positions with similar duties and responsibilities is a *job*.

The job results from the need for certain tasks to be performed. The tasks performed by a single worker should be similar in nature requiring essentially the same skills and abilities. It makes little sense to design a job consisting of two tasks, one of which is sweeping the floor while the other is operating a drill press. Job design begins from the consideration of what end result is required and then works backward to determine what tasks are necessary to achieve the required result. When all tasks are identified and defined, those that are similar can be grouped into a position or positions and, as defined previously, a group of positions requiring similar duties and responsibilities becomes a job.

When a job has been defined, standards for that job should be established. Of course the types of standards will vary depending upon the job. Very precise standards can be established in terms of time or output for a production job, while standards for a manager may be much less precise and even subjective. Nevertheless some standards should exist; otherwise it would be impossible to evaluate the performance of any employee. Even the president of the company is subject to job evaluation by the Board of Directors and the basis for that evaluation is his overall performance as exemplified by the so-called bottom line on the profit and loss statement.

Jobs are evaluated for the purpose of establishing a hierarchy of jobs which in turn is necessary for a balanced wage structure for the company. Various methods of job evaluation have been devised, but the three most common are job ranking, factor comparison, and the point rating system. We will discuss only the first of these since it is the simplest and is especially suited to the small or medium-sized business.

Job evaluation by the ranking method means, as the name indicates, the arranging of the various jobs in the order of their difficulty, responsibility and other requirements. The usual procedure is to identify the highest and the lowest jobs and then work gradually toward the jobs in the middle.

After jobs have been ranked, it is necessary to establish a wage structure based upon the ranking. It is not administratively feasible to have a different wage rate for each job, therefore, the list of jobs must be divided into a number of groups, each group containing jobs which are similar. A money value can then be assigned to each group.

The job ranking method can be used satisfactorily in evaluating positions that include numerous duties of a nonroutine nature and intangible factors that are not involved in production. Consequently, it is used a great deal for evaluating supervisory positions. Since job ranking is a relatively simple process, it is appropriate for small companies because it does not involve the complicated procedures and cost of the other systems.

The tendency in job design in recent years has been to de-skill jobs, that is, break them apart, routinize and automate them in order to improve productivity. This applies invariably to production jobs. Most recently however worker dissatisfaction with highly routine jobs has become increasingly evident. Instead of increasing productivity the result has often been that productivity has decreased due to tardiness, absenteeism and general worker dissatisfaction. Furthermore, the quality of the product has also declined. As a result, many companies have looked into methods that make the work more meaningful and to some degree integrate the worker into the decision-making process. One form of participatory management proposed was to have the organizational structure of the firm consist of overlapping work groups. At least one member of each work group was also a member of a work group at the next higher level in the organizational structure. In this way as information and directives originated at the higher levels, the lower levels in the structure were automatically apprised and did not have to depend on information working its way by memorandum or by directive through some complicated chain of command. In this type of organization, all workers in a group were responsible for decisions regarding the manner in which the group performed its functions.

Other less radical departures from traditional practices involve job enrichment and job enlargement. In job enrichment, each worker is responsible for a sequence of activities leading to the production of some significant element of the product or service rather than performing a single activity repetitively. In production, rather than have a job consist of merely tightening a single bolt on a subassembly, the job might be enriched to make a single worker responsible for assembling the entire component. The objective of job enrichment is to give the worker a greater opportunity to exercise his skills and to provide a more challenging occupation.

Job enlargement, has a similar goal as job enrichment. Generally job enlargement increases the number of different tasks that a single worker is responsible for. In that way it is similar to job enrichment. Another method used for job enlargement is to rotate workers among a variety of different tasks.

Not all types of jobs can be enriched or enlarged in order to increase worker satisfaction. Mixed results have been reported from different companies and industries on attempts to use one or more of these approaches. However, because of the importance of the human resource to an efficiently operated business organization, awareness by management of the worker's problems and feelings about his job and the various approaches to improving the worker's degree of satisfaction with his job have become a necessity.

WAGES AND BENEFITS

Wage determination is one of the most difficult and most important problems of management in the context of human resource management. It is of great significance to the workers and their families because their standard of living depends upon the wages they receive. The status of the worker within the factory and the standing of his family in the community also depend in part upon his earnings in relation to the earnings of others. Both the amount of wages paid and the method of payment are important. Social significance is attached to such distinctions as being on the office payroll and being paid by the week or month rather than by the hour.

To the employer the problem of wages is important not only because wages are a part of the cost of the product but also because an equitable and satisfactory settlement of the wage question is a factor in the establishment of good personnel relations. Controversies over wages are not the only cause of industrial strife, although they are a frequent cause. Furthermore, the wages paid by a firm can determine to large degree the type of applicants who seek employment there and the composition of the company's workforce. The company that wants to hire above-average employees must be willing to pay wages which are also above-average. The converse also holds true. If a company has a below-average wage scale, those who apply for work there will be persons who lack the ability to hold better jobs or who have been dismissed from other companies. It is unlikely that any company could recruit a satisfactory workforce under those circumstances.

Unless company management is willing to provide a wage scale satisfactory to its employees, it cannot expect that the workers will be motivated to give their best efforts. The objective of lower labor costs often diverts management's attention from the important goals of lower unit costs of labor and overhead. Increased productivity is not possible when those who are expected to provide it feel that they are being underpaid.

Management must also recognize that it has a responsibility for the economic improvement of its employees as well as the enhancement of owner's profits. An enterprise provides a satisfactory wage for its workforce only if it enables them to increase their standard of living. In an inflationary period a satisfactory wage refers to more than an increased amount of money wages, as the standard of living can only rise with a larger real wage. The real wage refers to the purchasing power of a money wage, which increases when wage increases surpass price increases. The payment of a satisfactory real wage should be a long-run management objective and can be achieved when workers are permitted to share in the increasing productivity of the company.

Practically, most employers establish wage rates by bargaining with employees either as individuals or collectively. The resulting wages do not necessarily relate to the contribution of the employee to the production of the product or service which constitutes the business of the company. When it is desirable to reward employees for exceptional contributions, managers should consider merit rating systems, bonuses, and profit-sharing plans.

Merit rating provides a technique for obtaining a more meaningful employee appraisal. It provides the factors which should be the basis of evaluation and a method to aid in determining the degree of each factor exhibited by each employee. Merit rating also has been called employee appraisal and efficiency rating. The objective of merit rating is to obtain some measure of the comparable accomplishments or the potentialities of employees.

Merit rating has been used primarily as the basis for granting wage increases within the rate range for a particular wage classification.

However, many companies have also used merit rating as the basis for the promotion of their employees. Evaluating the potential of employees for positions requiring greater responsibilities and skills can help management reduce the number of mistakes when promoting workers. A careful appraisal over a period of time can provide the information needed to make a proper choice when a promotion is necessary. This precludes hasty decisions based on insufficient information and reduces criticism that selection was based on favoritism.

Merit rating can also provide some indication concerning the success of a company's selection process and training program. If ratings of new workers on a job show that they are not capable of doing the work, they can be transferred to another department or discharged before the end of their probationary period. If this occurs frequently, it indicates that there are serious deficiencies in the selection process.

In profit sharing, the employee gets a share of the profit as an additional lump-sum payment on some periodic basis. The share due each employee may be paid in cash or in company stock.

The advantage to the employer of a profit-sharing plan is that it encourages a moderate degree of cooperation. In small companies, it has tended to break down the distinctions between crafts and to encourage workers to assist in any work that needs to be done. It gives workers a reason to be interested in the elimination of idle time of men and machines and in the reduction of spoilage and waste. It also usually results in a reduction in labor turnover.

Many companies that do not have a profit-sharing agreement regularly pay a bonus to their employees near the end of the year. The bonus is a gratuity, but the amount may be based upon annual wages or salaries. Employees are usually classified into groups according to the number of years of service, with the oldest employees receiving the largest bonuses.

Bonuses are designed to develop the loyalty of employees and to decrease labor turnover. Since the amount varies from year to year, employees cannot rely upon it as a means of meeting their obligations. If payments are made regularly, employees may regard the bonus as part of their wages.

Another important factor related to but not a part of employee wages is that of wage supplements or fringe benefits. In most companies these peripheral benefits account for approximately 30% of the cost of labor. Initially these benefits were provided by employers as goodwill gestures and morale boosters. Over the years, the number and types of fringe benefits have been increasing until they now represent a significant part of the employee's benefit package. In addition to vacation and sick leave, fringe benefits typically include employer contributions to retirement, life and health and accident insurance, maternity leaves, and educational benefits both for the employee and his dependents.

For the medium-sized and particularly the small business the proliferation of fringe benefits can represent a substantial cost. In unionized companies these benefits often result from the collective bargaining process. Once granted however they are difficult to rescind. An examination of the costs and benefits to the company of additional fringe benefits should be a part of the profit maximization program.

THE QUALITY OF THE WORKING ENVIRONMENT

The quality of work life is a function of the various factors discussed previously as well as other factors both tangible and intangible that are beyond the scope of this book. It is quite evident that a happy and motivated workforce is one of the most valuable assets that any business organization can have while the opposite can lead to profit erosion. It is also evident that the addition of various employee benefits will not necessarily lead to the desired conditions and that these benefits, being costly, can also lead to profit erosion.

In the context of profit maximization, when the initial checklist indicates that problems may exist in the human resource area, it becomes necessary for the manager to analyze the overall working environment to determine if conditions exist that contribute to worker dissatisfaction. A pleasant working environment is usually rather easy to achieve without large expenditures of funds. Clean, light, and pleasant work areas; convenient and well-maintained facilities; and probably above all a supportive and enlightened management philosophy are the ingredients that lead to a satisfied and effective labor force.

SUMMARY

The labor force, the human factor in the organization, represents the most important resource of the enterprise. It is also the most difficult resource to manage. Mathematical formulas and techniques so successful in other areas such as production control, inventory control, and quality control are all but useless in dealing with human beings. Without a competent, well-motivated, and satisfied workforce however all of the other techniques for profit maximization will be useless because the manager must depend upon human beings to apply them effectively and make them work. Although costs associated with labor generally represent the major portion of the company's operating costs, the difference between the expenditure necessary to obtain and maintain a competent and satisfied labor force and that which leads to the opposite is often small. Of course all proposed expenditures for employee benefits and compensation must be analyzed in terms of costs and benefits if profits are to be maximized. However, well-thought-out expenditures in this area generally provide returns that make them well worthwhile.

13. Information Systems and Computers

To this point we have completed the discussion of the major areas within the business where profit maximization techniques can be applied to halt profit erosion. We have also discussed certain tools that the manager can use to this end, cost and budgetary control and forecasting techniques. We have however saved for last the discussion of probably the most important managerial tool, that is, the computer based information system. None of the profit maximization techniques discussed in this book can be applied effectively without the availability of pertinent, accurate, current and timely information, in other words, without the use of an efficient management information system.

Profit maximization requires that the manager make decisions regarding business operations in the areas discussed previously. Effective decision making depends on the acquisition and proper interpretation of information. Consequently, the manager uses information as an aid to decision making, not as an end in itself.

There is certainly no lack of data applicable to managerial decisions. Large quantities of money and enormous numbers of manhours are expended searching for, gathering, processing, analyzing and transmitting information. These expenditures are generally worthwhile, since information is indeed the raw material of management. Recent advances in information technology have increased the efficiency of this process by providing more data in less time and at a lower cost than ever before. However, this has not been accomplished without creating new and serious problems for the manager who not only must cope with the flood of information but is expected to use it advantageously. Today, one of the greatest problems faced by the manager is not one of obtaining information, but rather one of obtaining *proper* information and then *knowing what to do with it.*

If decision making is the principal function of management and information is its raw material, then the increased availability of data should be desirable. However, distinguishing between data that are pertinent and those that are not, and knowing what to do with the former, is not always easy. Utilizing information properly requires knowledge and skill. We have been discussing techniques dependent upon the availability of information. In this chapter we will consider the system required to provide this information in the right place and at the right time.

INFORMATION SYSTEMS

The successful application of the tools and techniques of profit maximization is highly dependent upon the availability of accurate, pertinent and timely information. Advances in the area of small computers and significant reduction in their costs have made the computer an almost indispensable tool even to the small business organization.

It has often been said the principal function of a manager is to make decisions while the principal function of everyone else is to provide him with the information that he needs to do so. To a degree this is quite true. In order to make the decisions required to optimize operations in those areas critical to profit maximization, information about those operations must be available. However, hand gathering and processing of information is slow, tedious and frequently inaccurate. The computer and the related information system can be the solution.

Many advances in the production, communication, analysis and processing of information have been made recently. These advances have taken place in two general areas which we can refer to as hardware and software. Hardware refers to the machines which process information. Software is a broad term that can be used to include the techniques and procedures by which both machines and human beings process information. In fact, the term software can encompass not only computer programs and languages but also the set of analytical techniques that are used to operate upon raw data and to derive intelligence from it. An information system consists of both hardware and software components and human beings. In fact, hardware, software, and human beings accumulating, processing, and analyzing data are all valuable sources of information useful to the executive. But in order to perform their functions effectively and achieve their objectives, the individual tools must be coordinated and integrated into a total system called a *management information system*. A management information system is simply a combination of people, machines and procedures designed to provide information to management. However, without the systems approach, each of the individual components could be working at cross purposes to one another or to no single purpose at all. Duplication, waste and inefficiency could be the result.

The term management information system, abbreviated MIS, is often thought to be synonymous with a data processing system comprised of an electronic digital computer together with its related hardware and software. It is implied that all management information systems are built around and utilize computers. This is not necessarily true. The management information system is simply a system for providing information and processing support for all of the management functions of an organization. The concept of such a system predates the advent of the computer by many years. However, computers have made the information system concept feasible and contributed significantly to its implementation. Without the digital computer, the MIS would be a great deal less effective.

OBTAINING INFORMATION

Everyone knows, or should know, that business managers must constantly make decisions. This is true whether the business is a large, multinational corporation or a small convenience market in a suburban shopping center. Everyone also knows that in order to make effective decisions, the decision maker needs information. Decision making without information might just as well be accomplished by tossing a coin. On the basis of the previous statements, you might conclude that the more information available to the manager, the easier it will be to make decisions and the better the results. However, this conclusion is not necessarily correct. More is not always better.

Information is not only valuable for decision making, it is necessary. In fact *proper* information is absolutely indispensable in the decision-making process. Notice the emphasis on the word proper. Inappropriate, outdated, and erroneous information can be as detrimental to good decision making and consequently to profit maximization as current, accurate, and pertinent information is beneficial. Unfortunately, most managers, the users of information, can't be sure whether the information provided to them represents the former or the latter. In order to be able to distinguish between good and bad information it is necessary to understand how information is obtained as data and what is done to it on the way to the executive's desk.

Although the words information and data are frequently used interchangeably and do in fact have similar dictionary definitions, we will differentiate between the two for our own purposes. *Data* is a collective noun referring to a set of facts. These facts or data may consist of words, numbers, or symbols or a combination of any or all of these. The singular of data is *datum* and means a single fact or one item from the set of data. Numerical data are called *statistics*.

Any set of data contains information, but not necessarily in usable form. In fact, the information content of a set of data is usually not immediately apparent. In order to obtain information from data, processing is usually required. Information can be obtained from data by a process that could include rearrangement, organization, computation and other operations. *Information then is data presented in a form useful for decision making.* In fact, the purpose of all data processing is to obtain information from data.

Occasionally data need no processing to convert it to information. This may be true when the transaction which generates the data is a simple one. In most instances however a great deal of processing is required. This is where the computer based information system becomes almost indispensable.

THE ELECTRONIC DIGITAL COMPUTER

It is virtually impossible to discuss the topic of information and modern information processing without discussing, at least briefly, the electronic digital computer. This device stands at the heart of every modern information processing system. Although debatable, a case could be made for the statement that of all the technological developments that have occurred since World War II, the electronic digital computer is the one that has made the greatest impact on our society.

Probably less debatable is the enormous impact this device has had on business organizations. A claim could be made that the tremendous growth of many large corporations was made possible by the computer. However, our purpose is not to discuss the impact of the computer on business or society but to explain what a computer is and what it can and cannot do.

There are many common misconceptions about computers. These include the two extreme views that a computer is nothing more than a very large and fast adding machine on the one hand, or that it is a semihuman entity capable of thinking as humans think, on the other.

While there is some truth in both viewpoints, neither is totally correct. By explaining what a computer is and how it works we hope to dispel some of these misconceptions and provide the manager with a better understanding of this device which can be depended on for much necessary decision-making information. Of course, the user of the information output of an electronic data processing system need not be an expert in computer science any more than the driver of a motor vehicle needs a degree in engineering. However, in order to use this tool most effectively, it is necessary for the user to have at least a basic understanding of computers and how they work.

We use the term *computer* to refer to those pieces of hardware that perform certain data processing functions. This machine uses electronic circuitry to manipulate symbols in a predetermined way. A computer therefore is a device capable of manipulating data and solving problems by performing certain prescribed mathematical and logical operations.

There are two general types of electronic computers. These are *analog computers* and *digital computers*. The analog computer uses electronic circuits to construct a physical model, or analog, of a process or system. Analog computers are useful in engineering problem solving but are not particularly applicable to the type of data processing required in business. The digital computer on the other hand manipulates discrete symbols such as numbers. This ability is what makes digital computers so useful in processing the type of data generated by business transactions and used for managerial decision making.

WHAT COMPUTERS CAN AND CANNOT DO

The electronic digital computer is a powerful and versatile tool for processing data. However, its capabilities are not without limits. A manager must know these capabilities and limits to make the most effective and efficient use of the processing system.

As mentioned above, there are two very common but divergent views held by laymen about the computer. One is the belief that a computer is a giant brain endowed with human or semihuman qualities. In other words, it is a machine that can think. The other view is that computers are simply enormous calculating machines similar to the common handheld calculators and differing from them only in size.

A great deal of the difference between these two conflicting views is simply a matter of semantics, the meaning of words. For example, what do we mean by the *brain* and how do we define thinking or thought? For that matter, what do we mean by words like smart and stupid?

The computer is of course a machine. It is not human nor does it resemble a human being. This computing machine or computer manipulates symbols according to a set of instructions within a logical framework provided by a human operator. Within that framework, the computer can manipulate those symbols more accurately and a great deal more quickly than any human is capable of doing. However, the logic that directs the symbol manipulation is human logic.

The computer can think only in the sense that it can follow the step-by-step instructions stored in its memory. The imputation of human characteristics to the computer probably results from the use of words such as *memory* to describe one of its major components, *read* to refer to the process of receiving data from an input device, and *learn* to refer to the capability that some computers have to improve some aspect of their performance by a trial-and-error analysis of past results. This is somewhat similar to the common practice of humanizing inanimate things as seen in references to seagoing vessels by the feminine pronoun *she* and in assigning human names to hurricanes and tropical storms for no logical reason.

However, within limits the results of the computer's operation are the same as the results of a thought process. Consequently, in this sense, the computer is capable of "thinking." Furthermore, the difference between a large digital computer and a small, handheld calculator involves more than simply size and speed. The ability to store instructions in its own memory, execute those instructions without human intervention, and perform logical operations in addition to arithmetic, makes it a great deal more than a large calculating machine.

In support of the giant brain view of computers, proponents frequently call attention to the fact that computers have been programmed to play games like tic-tac-toe, checkers and chess. And what's more, they have been able to improve their own performance and beat their human mentors consistently. Dr. A. L. Samuels of IBM developed a program to teach a computer to play checkers. After playing a large number of games, the computer could consistently beat Dr. Samuels. However, the logic for playing the game and improving performance by trial and error was provided by the human programmer. The computer could learn to play a better game, but only because its instructions showed it how to do so.

Of course, from the viewpoint of the user of the computer, a discussion of whether a computer can think or learn or has intelligence is a matter of academic interest only. So long as the computer and its related system components provide him with accurate and timely information in a useful form, the rest has little importance. It is much more important for the manager to be familiar with the capabilities and limitations of the computer so that he can use it most effectively. It can be extremely frustrating to demand and expect more from a system than it is capable of providing.

The computer can only process the data provided for it. If those data are inaccurate, out of date, or irrelevant to the problem at hand, no amount of processing can keep the end result from being inaccurate, out of date or irrelevant. A common acronym that describes such a situation is GIGO, meaning garbage-in/garbage-out. Avoiding garbage-in is the responsibility of the manager. Only he knows exactly what information he needs, and consequently he must specify precisely not only what that is but how and where it should be obtained.

TIME SHARING AND MULTIPROGRAMMING

For the small or even medium-sized business, extensive computer capabilities can often be obtained by time sharing or multiprogramming. Multiprogramming means that several different jobs can be processed by the computer at virtually the same time. Whenever there is a natural pause or delay in processing one job, another is brought into the CPU (central processing unit) and executed so that no computer time is wasted. Jobs waiting for processing are maintained in a queue while output is maintained in a similar queue. When the operating system needs another job, it is selected from the input queue sequentially, according to some system of priority scheduling.

The computer's operation in multiprogramming is controlled by a sophisticated set of instructions called an *executive program*. This program causes the computer to receive input from several sources simultaneously, putting unprocessed data into temporary secondary storage until the previous jobs have been processed. The computer's central processing unit is automatically moved from job to job as the appropriate program is brought into primary storage to process the associated data. Each job is retained in the CPU until its processing is complete. Work starts on the next job only when the previous job has been completed or if the first job has been interrupted either for output or for more input. Whenever such an interruption occurs, the CPU is immediately shifted to the next job in the queue.

Time sharing is a special type of multiprogramming in which the time each job is allowed to remain in the CPU on any one turn is limited. When a job has been in the CPU for the allotted time, an interrupt is initiated by the executive program and the job is transferred to secondary storage in order to allow the next job in the queue to enter the CPU. The amount of time allocated to each job on a single turn is called a *time slice*.

Time sharing provides multiple users with computing time on a periodic basis. Each user can access the computer through remote terminals without any extensive knowledge about computer hardware or programming. Although each user shares the computer with others, the computer switches among programs so rapidly that there is little or no delay in providing each user with his completed job.

In a time sharing system, the user may access programs and data that are already in the computer or may enter new programs and data through a terminal. Instructions and data are input to the computer through a keyboard and output is received either as a hard copy printout or as a display on a cathode ray tube (CRT) screen.

With time sharing and a remote terminal, managers are able to communicate directly with the computer and avoid the use of intermediaries. Consequently, many sources of error and/or data distortion due to human communication problems can be eliminated. All the manager needs is a terminal and the ability to use it.

Recently, large computer systems have been developed that utilize time sharing principles and in which the computer becomes a type of communications center. Many different input and output devices and terminals are connected to the central computer from remote locations by means of cables or telephone lines. Such large-scale systems give smaller companies and organizations the advantage of having access to large computers without the cost of buying or leasing such a system for their own exclusive use.

CLASSIFYING DIGITAL COMPUTERS

A common method of classifying digital computers is by size. Generally five classes are identified. These are microcomputers, minicomputers, small, medium, and large computers. These classes are somewhat arbitrary and to some extent overlapping. There is no universal consensus as to exactly what characteristics define each of the classes. However, these categories do provide a useful means of grouping the different types of computers currently available. Because new computers are appearing on the market constantly and prices are continually changing we will not refer to any particular brand of computer nor will we attempt to fix or estimate prices.

Microcomputers are the smallest and least expensive of the computers on the market. These computers are primarily intended for use as personal computers in the home, small office or small business. Microcomputers began to appear on the market in the early 1970s although the earliest of this type entered the market in 1969.

A microcomputer system consists of a central processing unit about the size of stereo speaker cabinet, a keyboard for entering data, and a video display which is about the size of a table model television receiver. Although characterized by the term *micro* these systems are by no means portable in the commonly accepted sense of that word.

If a typewriter is substituted for the simple keyboard, the microcomputer can provide a hard copy printout in addition to, or instead of, the video display. For faster printout, a separate printer can be added to the system.

The internal memory or primary storage unit of a microcomputer is relatively small. However, if necessary, it can be expanded by the addition of slower secondary storage units.

One step above the microcomputers in size is the minicomputer. Minicomputers are compact systems sometimes referred to as desk top computers.

Minicomputers may use magnetic tape or discs for data entry in addition to keyboards. However, the tape and disc drives are smaller and slower than those used with larger computers. Limited input and output capabilities constitute one of the disadvantages of minicomputers. Most have only one input and one output device. Other disadvantages include limited storage capacity and limited flexibility. Offsetting these disadvantages is the fact that minicomputers require no special installation provisions while large computers sometimes need special flooring, air conditioning, and humidity and dust control. The combination of low cost and easy installation are advantages which make the minicomputer suitable for small organizations that do not require large storage capacity and fast processing speeds.

A computer system is usually considered to be small when it has a single input device and one or two output devices. Small computers achieve flexibility through a modular design and are capable of growing by adding memory capacity, input/output devices and other peripheral equipment. Consequently, the actual cost depends upon the options selected.

Because of their modular design, small computers have greater potential than do the minicomputers and are well-suited to small and medium-sized businesses that prefer having their own system to the time-sharing approach. Even larger organizations with a medium or large computer may find it advantageous to augment it with one or more small computers. The small computers are then used to handle jobs that do not require the speed and power of the larger models.

Medium-sized computers can handle more complicated functions and process data more rapidly than the small computer. Because of their power, their ability to process data more rapidly, and their large internal storage capacity, medium computers are adequate to meet the needs of most business organizations.

Today's large computers can be afforded only by very large organizations whose data processing requirements are so great that they can keep these giant computer systems busy. Although very expensive to own or lease, due to their speed and power, the per unit cost of data processing on these machines is very low provided there is sufficient work to avoid idle machine time. Government agencies and large corporations are among the types of organizations that can use these large computers cost effectively. However, smaller organizations can utilize the power of these machines on a time-sharing basis as discussed previously.

THE MANAGEMENT INFORMATION SYSTEM

Hardware, software, and human beings accumulating, processing, and analyzing data are all valuable tools for obtaining information useful to managers in profit maximization. However, in order to perform their functions effectively and achieve their objectives, these individual tools must be coordinated and integrated into a total system called a *management information system*. A management information system is simply a combination of people, machines, and procedures designed to provide information to management.

Organizations of all types—industrial, governmental, or other—have always required systems for the collection, processing, storage, retrieval and dissemination of data. In fact, the single most essential ingredient of effective management is current and accurate information, a fact that we have previously emphasized. Information is central to all organized activity. The contribution made by the MIS is the integration of the many unrelated information subsystems in the organization into a single system that focuses on the information requirements of the organization as a whole rather than on the individual needs of its component parts. The computer adds a new and powerful tool to the information system concept. With the computer and its electronic adjuncts, information processing, flow and dissemination can be accomplished much more quickly and accurately than in a system based on hand or electromechanical processing. This means that more information of higher quality and currency can be at the disposal of managers for use in their function as decision makers.

A management information system is an integrated, man-machine system whose purpose is to provide information to support the operations, management, and decision-making functions in an organization. The system usually consists of computer hardware and software, operating procedures, management and decision models, and a data base.

Managers have always recognized the need for pertinent information. In the past however they were forced to rely on various uncoordinated sources. Each manager then processed the data on a personal basis, and consequently each worked under different perceptions about his operating environment. The advent of the computer based information system changed all this. The modern MIS has altered the management process from one that utilized guesswork, piecemeal information and isolated problem solving to one using sophisticated data processing, systems information, and systems problem solving. Whereas managers previously relied on various individual sources of information, MIS provides a total information system. Consequently the system as a whole has become a much more powerful tool than the sum of its individual parts for assisting managers in solving problems and making decisions. By providing a common set of information it truly integrates the operations of the organization in such a way that the company is now viewed as an overall system with all its elements and components working toward a common objective.

MIS DESIGN AND STRUCTURE

The overall design and the resulting structure of a management information system is based on the requirements and objectives of the organization. Information systems may be very extensive or they may be limited depending upon those considerations. The initial step in MIS design is to determine what the information requirements and the objectives of management really are. The resulting management information system will only be as effective as the specification of these objectives and requirements is accurate and complete. Large sums of money and great amounts of time and effort can be wasted on designing and implementing information systems that generate unneeded and useless information.

After identifying what the information requirements of the system users are, it is then necessary to determine the sources from which the information or data will be obtained. Data can be obtained from both internal and external sources. Data from external sources usually result from a planned search or survey designed to obtain information related to some specific management decision situation. These are often unique, one-of-a-kind situations, and the information required is not needed on a continuous basis. Although the MIS must be capable of handling the requirements which result from such unique situations, it is most usually concerned with data generated internally on a periodic or continuing basis.

The function of the organization's information system is to provide the information necessary to analyze operations and to perform the profit maximization techniques previously described. This is not to imply that profit maximization is the only reason for having a management information system. Information is a valuable resource to the organization. Like other resources such as labor, material, money, space, etc., it must be managed effectively. However, in the present context we are concerned with the MIS and its impact on a profit maximization program.

In actuality the management information system is really a set of smaller information systems or subsystems. These include but are not limited to a financial information system, a personnel information system, a marketing information system, a purchasing information system and a manufacturing information system. In various firms other information systems may exist or some of the above might be combined. In addition, the manufacturing information system might include several other information subsystems such as the quality subsystem, the production subsystem and the inventory subsystem. In some organizations the purchasing subsystem might also be included under the manufacturing information system. A discussion of the various information systems and subsystems pertinent to the profit maximization program follows.

The Marketing Information System

The marketing information system provides data on the demand for and satisfaction with the company's products or services. The information provided by this system impinges on the profit maximization program in several ways. First, marketing information is essential for performing the forecasting function. An accurate forecast of demand is needed for capacity planning, inventory control, efficient purchasing, production control and staffing. Furthermore, this information system should include data regarding customer satisfaction or dissatisfaction with the company's products or services. Complaints, ill will and lost business are all indications of possible profit erosion. Information provided in this area indicates the quality of the company's product and performance and should interface with the quality information subsystem.

The marketing information system may consist of any or all of the following subsystems:

1. The market research subsystem
2. The distribution subsystem
3. The advertising and promotion subsystem
4. The sales subsystem
5. The price subsystem
6. The competition subsystem
7. The customer subsystem

Each of these subsystems gather and compile information regarding some aspect of the marketing system. However, the fact that the overall marketing information system can be divided into subsystems categorized by type of marketing information does not imply that these subsystems are separate and independent of one another. The design of the marketing information system requires the integration of the individual subsystems into a single comprehensive information system for marketing data.

The Financial Information System

The accounting system provides a record of the firm's financial transactions over time. Each day thousands of transactions occur within the organization and between the organization and other organizations external to it. Consequently, the sheer volume of data requires a great deal of processing before they can be put into a form that is useful to management. The way in which these data are processed and analyzed determines how they will be used in the profit maximization program. The financial information system also consists of several subsystems. These include the fixed asset accounting subsystem, the payroll subsystem, the accounts receivable and accounts payable subsystems, the funds management subsystem and the financial control subsystem. The integrated financial information system interfaces with all of the other information systems that comprise the MIS. In terms of profit maximization, it directly affects cost and budgetary control, capacity planning, inventories, and human resources.

The Production Information Systems

Production in this context refers to the production of the commodity that the firm sells to its customers. If the commodity is a product, production may involve manufacturing. Of course if the organization simply provides goods for resale, then manufacturing would not be involved. If the commodity produced is a service, again manufacturing would not be involved. However, in the sense that every profit-making business is a production system with inputs, processes, and outputs, every profitable business should have a production information system.

Similar to the other major information systems in the organization, the production information system consists of several major subsystems. These could include the inventory subsystem, the purchasing subsystem, the quality subsystem, and in a manufacturing organization, the manufacturing subsystem. The latter is probably the most complex of the production systems since it is concerned with information regarding all aspects of the manufacturing process that convert the inputs of material, labor and capital into the finished product. Taken as a whole, the production information system is vital to the profit maximization techniques relating to inventory, purchasing, quality control and production control.

The Personnel Information System

This system is the repository for all information about the human resources of the company. Records should be maintained on all currently employed personnel as well as on the sources of potential new employees. These records should include information on the education, skills, current position, age, sex, and the wages or salary of each employee as well as performance evaluations and promotability.

In conjunction with forecasts, projections of personnel requirements can be made and the availability of personnel both internal and external to the company can be estimated. The personnel information subsystem should also contain data pertaining to wage rates, benefits, union contracts, and so on for other companies of similar size and in the same industry.

THE MANAGER AND THE INFORMATION SYSTEM

Numerous decisions are required of a manager every day. Each decision process can be viewed as the transformation of information inputs into decision outputs. Consequently, the manager as well as the system designer and analyst should be concerned with three distinct phases of the decision process. These are the information inputs needed for the decision, the decision process itself, and the decision outputs and their implementation. It is fairly easy to formalize routine decisions. A decision model can be devised and expressed as a series of mathematical equations in the computer program. However, nonroutine, one-of-a-kind decisions are much more difficult to formalize. These are frequently based on qualitative considerations and the subjective judgments of the decision maker rather than on formalized mathematical models. Nevertheless, accurate and current information is still vital to the decision process and continued advances in information technology and decision theory are providing solutions to problems previously considered unmanageable. The effect of the management information system on the job of the manager results from the capabilities of computer systems to supply management information. Three specific capabilities of these systems have had a significant impact on the practice of management. These are speed, accuracy, and the ability to perform extremely complex analyses.

The ability of the computer to perform hundreds of thousands of calculations in fractions of a second has an obvious impact on management. Data can be summarized, analyzed, checked and reported rapidly thus shortening the management control cycle significantly. Furthermore the accuracy of the data can be relied on. If properly programmed, the computer is unlikely to make any mistakes, which is not always true of its human operators and the other human components of a man-machine system. Of course, as we have discussed previously, computers do only what they are instructed to do. If they are programmed improperly, then errors can occur. However, if the system is designed to enter data accurately and process them correctly, the output should also be correct and accurate.

With a modern management information system available, managers now have at their disposal such tools for decision making as operations research, statistics, mathematics and decision analyis. It is not unusual for optimal production schedules to be developed by computers applying the techniques of mathematical programming. Work schedules and product development programs are being developed using critical path analysis. Investment and other financial decisions are being guided by complex analyses of mathematical models. With the computer based MIS, developing problems can be recognized early and corrected before losses are incurred. Sales, advertising, inventory, production and practically every other facet of the organization benefits by the evaluation of decision problems on a routine basis that would only be possible because of the availability of the computer.

The implications of these capabilities for the manager are obvious. In order to compete effectively with their counterparts in other companies and industries, managers must be able to utilize all information and analytical tools. They need not be mathematicians, statisticians, or operations researchers, but they should be aware of the available tools and be able to use them. They must also have sufficient knowledge to be able to assure that they are receiving competent advice and technical assistance in applying and in interpreting these various analytical procedures. The manager must not fall into the trap of abrogating his responsibilities by depending entirely on the specialists and so-called experts. To the specialist, all problems are viewed from the perspective of his specialty. Problems tend to be narrowly defined and often are incompletely analyzed. Unwarranted assumptions are often made. Unless the manager knows enough about the tools and the language of the specialist to ask the proper questions, to participate in the development of the analytical models and to check the results, the outcome in terms of his job performance is likely to be inadequate.

The implementation of an MIS in the organization assumes that the manager involved is familiar enough with the concept to use it in performing his managerial and decision-making functions. This in turn implies that training in the concept and use of the MIS constitutes an important facet of its implementation. However, no matter how effective the MIS may be, it is not a substitute for competent managers exercising their own judgment and applying their managerial expertise to the solution of problems.

In the final analysis, it is the information needs of the manager that establish the parameters of the management information systems. The purpose of the MIS is to provide the manager with the information he needs to perform his functions most effectively. Consequently, it is the information requirements of the manager that establish the parameters of the system. In order for the system to be effective and efficient, the user must make these requirements known during the design of the system and then must continually evaluate the system's performance in meeting these requirements. In order to do this, the manager must be both knowledgeable and involved. However, once the management information system is in place and operating, it will simplify the manager's job significantly. And in the execution of a profit maximization program, such a system is indispensable.

14. Concluding the Profit Maximization Program

In a very real sense, there is no conclusion to a profit maximization program. Profit maximization must be a continuing activity, reviewing operations in all departments constantly in order to detect and remedy incidents of profit erosion. Therefore, even though the program has been completed, and the tools, techniques, and procedures discussed in the preceding chapters have been applied successfully, the manager cannot afford to be complacent. One of Murphy's Laws states that whenever something can go wrong, it will. Nowhere is this more true than in the operation of a business.

Continuous surveillance of the operations of the business is one of the functions of the manager. In this respect, the checklist is an indispensable tool. By using the checklist on a periodic basis, changing conditions can be detected promptly. And although changes can represent improvements, they can also signal a deterioration or decline in some activity that could lead to or be a source of profit erosion.

The initial application of the maximization techniques discussed here is simply a beginning. In order to maximize profits over the long run, the process must continue over the life of the business. Maximum profits in one quarter or period and less than maximum profits in the ensuing periods would not represent a successful profit maximization program. To refer to the boat analogy one more time, once the leaks have been discovered and repaired, the repairs must be maintained and surveillance of new possible sources of leakage must be continued.

Although the previous chapters have outlined in some detail the basic techniques of profit maximization in such areas as inventories, production control, quality control, and so on, the manager need not always apply those techniques himself. As discussed in Chapter 2, the effective manager is an efficient delegator. Competent and well-trained subordinates are essential to the success of any business regardless of its size. Of course, the manager or entrepreneur of a one-man business has no subordinates to whom to delegate. But the one-man business doesn't usually exist for a very long period of time. Either it grows or it fails. If it grows, the problem of delegation of duties and authority and the training of competent subordinates must be addressed. If it fails, such discussions are purely academic.

Of course delegation does not relieve the manager of responsibility. Even if the actual profit maximization activities are implemented by others, the manager must still understand the concepts and be familiar with the methods of application and their operation. Without this understanding, the manager will never know if they are being applied properly and appropriately.

In writing a book on profit maximization for managers of small and medium-sized businesses, we did not specify the criteria for inclusion in or exclusion from these two categories. We leave that decision to the reader. In fact, this book is written for anyone who can benefit from reading it. If the benefit is significant, one-man businesses can become small businesses with multiple employees, small businesses can grow to be medium-sized, and medium-sized businesses can theoretically become large, no matter how those terms are defined.

Index

DATE DUE

FEB 14 1997	
MAR 1 2 2003	

BRODART, CO.   Cat. No. 23-221-003